THE ART OF THE EMPIRE STRIKES BACK ™

TEXT BY
VIC BULLUCK AND VALERIE HOFFMAN

EDITED BY
DEBORAH CALL

ART DIRECTION AND DESIGN
VIGON, NAHAS, VIGON

A DEL REY® BOOK

BALLANTINE BOOKS · NEW YORK

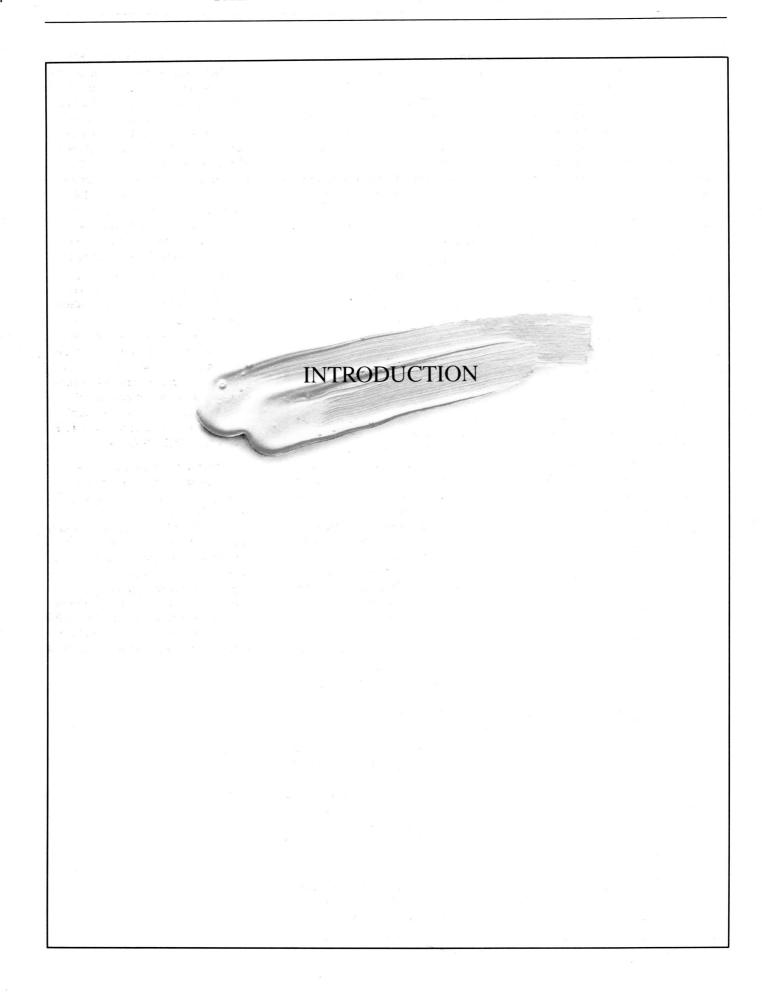

INTRODUCTION

t is not surprising to find filmgoers intensely arguing the merits of an actor, director, editor or cameraman of a film but even the most sophisticated audiences are not aware of the immense cinematic contribution made by artists and designers. They are the link between the script and the film technicians who transform the storyteller's imagination into reality.

As early as November of 1977, when a rough draft of THE EMPIRE STRIKES BACK was finished, Ralph McQuarrie and Joe Johnston began working on rough sketches for the new vehicles and characters that would appear in the film. Their work continued into the production of the film and they were joined at ILM by Johnston's assistant, Nilo Rodis-Jamero. George Lucas established ILM in Marin County to insure a home base for the technical high quality he demands in his films. It has since become a work haven for some of America's best young special effects personnel.

When the designs were fairly well established, McQuarrie began thumbnail sketches in which he played with various angles for viewing the central elements on screen. These sketches were preliminary to his production paintings which depict key scenes from the script. These paintings were used primarily to aid the production crew in the building of models, sets and costumes. They became a general reference point for everyone involved in the making of THE EMPIRE STRIKES BACK for the paintings helped to establish the mood of the film.

Simultaneously, Joe Johnston and Nilo Rodis-Jamero began to outline the action of the film in a series of detailed storyboard sketches, framed in the ratio by which the film was to be shot.

Whenever there was either a change in the script or a scene involving a special effects shot that didn't work, Johnston and Rodis-Jamero would sketch a new storyboard. Sometimes they redrew whole sequences. Most of the walls of Joe and Nilo's room at ILM are covered with storyboards. "These are only half the boards," Johnston smiled. "We just haven't put the other half up yet. When we do they'll go around the other side of the room and cover all the walls. And these boards just represent the work done involving models, matte paintings, or visual effects."

Only part of THE EMPIRE STRIKES BACK was done at ILM. A large number of storyboards were also drawn to guide the camera work of the live-action sequences that were filmed at EMI Elstree Studios in England. These storyboards were sketched by Ivor Beddoes.

The storyboards and production paintings were then given to the production designer. Although these gave him the scale and general look of the different sets, more detailing was required before each set could be built. This often meant that for practical reasons, changes in the original concept were necessary. It was the job of production designer, Norman Reynolds, to create functional stages for the actors, and design sets discussed or referred to in the script that had not been included in the production paintings. Reynolds also created all of the details which individually might have gone unnoticed but were necessary to achieve a realistic effect in the settings.

So, too, with costumes. John Mollo, costume designer, elaborated on the various sketches and paintings prepared in California, and made the actors' clothing and accessories functional.

The unique job of building the special alien creatures was handled by Stuart Freeborn. Most of his time was devoted to Yoda, the Tauntaun, the Ice Creature and revitalizing Chewbacca. Phil Tippett sculpted the clay miniatures of the Tauntaun which were used by Freeborn as a guide for the full size version. Fellow stop-motion animator, Jon Berg, worked extensively on the inner workings of the Empire's All Terrain Armored Transport.

In live action or miniatures, the final look of many scenes in THE EMPIRE STRIKES BACK depended upon the matte painters. Very early in production, decisions were made as to which sets could be built practically and which settings would be created in part or in whole with matte paintings. Harrison Ellenshaw, Ralph McQuarrie and Mike Pangrazio used the production paintings, storyboards and live action as a guide in their work to decide what portion of the frame would be matted, and then painted on a piece of glass to create the desired illusion.

Many production elements went into the making of THE EMPIRE STRIKES BACK. An inter-continental effort, it required the working cooperation of hundreds of people. This brief summary of the role of the artist understates the complexity of their interdependence as well as their constant communication with all involved with the production. Artists were essential to the creation of THE EMPIRE STRIKES BACK.

Director Irvin Kershner commented on the artists' contribution to the making of THE EMPIRE STRIKES BACK: "My concern in directing a picture is in telling a story and making the characters work within that context. In turn, the artists translate ideas into reality. They not only help make a vague idea concrete but they also bring color and texture to the film in the same way that a director brings life to it. All of these elements combine until elegance and drama are achieved."

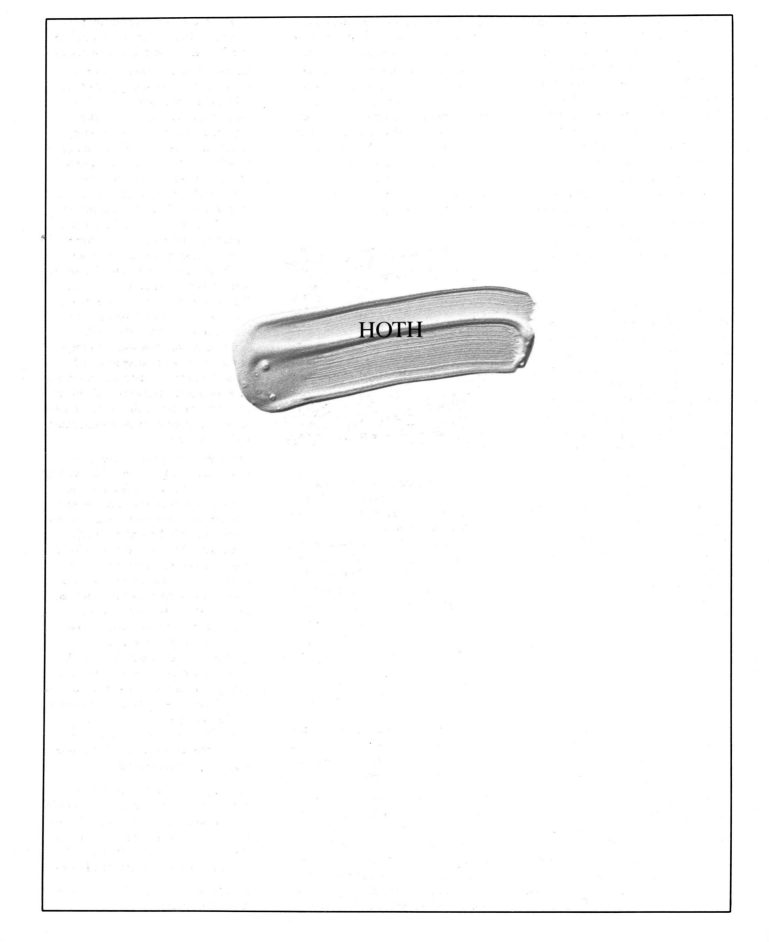

HOTH

After the destruction of the Empire's Death Star, the Rebels are relentlessly pursued by Darth Vader and his fleet of Imperial Star Destroyers. Luke Skywalker, Princess Leia, Han Solo, Chewbacca, See-Threepio, Artoo-Detoo and fellow Rebels unite on Hoth, a frozen piece of tundra spinning through space on the outer fringes of a distant galaxy.

The Rebels have blasted into the frozen landscape and created huge caverns to provide them with shelter from Hoth's harsh environment. Rebel scouting parties routinely explore the vast windswept plains and search for signs of life or any other presence on the planet.

Everything designed for the scenes on Hoth in THE EMPIRE STRIKES BACK had to depict the feeling of a frozen wilderness. The clothing had to look as if it could provide protection from the cold. Quilted fabrics and parkalike jackets with fur-lined hoods seemed appropriate. Energy packs with life-support capabilities were added to the gear the Rebels carried whenever away from their base. Breather hoods were created for the weather-proofed stormtrooper costumes. Hoth's creatures would need a thick layer of protective fat and fur. The heavy body of the Imperial All Terrain Armored Transport was designed to be supported by strong legs with a wide base to provide a distribution of weight for movement upon Hoth's icy crust. Since landspeeders on Hoth would be impractical, a wedge-shaped snowspeeder was designed to easily maneuver in the strong winds of Hoth.

Good ideas for the planning of Hoth, as elsewhere, were taken where they could be found and this meant tapping the minds of all the artists working on the film.

Many ideas were exchanged during the development of the Tauntaun and several people were involved in the process. The Tauntaun was first conceived of as a fierce, hairless reptile, then an ostrichlike mammal and later a vicious rodentlike animal. This sensitive and cognizant animal evolved into a furry, steedlike creature. Animated

by Phil Tippett, the Tauntaun is also a creature of significant importance in the field of stop-motion animation.

The script called for the Tauntaun to be running in almost all of its shots, which could be very difficult using a stop-motion technique. Stop-motion animation is similar to the effect that would be created by shooting many still pictures and running them through a projector at a very fast shutter speed. Each frame contains a single, crystal sharp image and when

the film is projected a funny kind of staccato movement is produced. A running horse in a motion picture appears to be real because the motion picture film inadequately captures the movement, and the legs therefore are blurred. Simulating the blurring effect in stop-motion adds to the realism. To achieve this effect the Tauntaun model was moved during the shooting of each frame. Each time the shutter of the camera opened to shoot one frame, the Tauntaun puppet was moved physically. This technique, never done before in the field of stop-motion animation, was accomplished by using a computerized track to free the animator's hands and give him more time to concentrate on the creature's subtler gestures and movements.

The All Terrain Armored Transport (AT-AT), fondly known as the walker, is an Imperial attack vehicle fifty feet high and functions as the centerpiece for many spectacular battle sequences in the film. The actual construction of such a monstrous machine to scale was found to be impractical. The realistic

look of the walkers created in miniature in the film is a credit to the ILM special effects artists and technicians.

Lucas felt the combination of the walker's mechanical design with its animallike movements would have a very ominous effect. The walker appears to move as if it were a large animal stalking prey. Initially designed by Joe Johnston, the outer appearance of the body and head took its final shape while under construction in the model shop at ILM. Engineering the AT-AT into an operational stop-motion model was the pet project of Jon Berg, who was responsible for the inner working patterns and animation of the walker. Various large animals were filmed and their leg movements analyzed in order to lend their characteristic movements to the model walkers. At the same time, prototype models were also videotaped and filmed in order to study various movement problems. But even with all the pre-planning, it was the models themselves that eventually determined their style of locomotion.

The walkers originally were to be filmed separately and then matted into the live action footage from the location shooting in Norway. As the test footage was developed, Lucas was disappointed with the shallow image created by shooting the white AT-AT models against a white snow background. This caused a temporary setback to all the work that had been done on the walker battle sequence over a period of two years. No one wanted a compromise in the sequence's visual impact. To solve the problem, Lucas turned to a talented young artist named Mike Pangrazio to paint realistic snow landscapes. These background paintings could be matched up with the live-action plate to give the sequence the added visual impact that was necessary.

To complete the effect, Nilo Rodis-Jamero built miniature snow sets to fill out the landscape. Using an elaborate system of pulleys, wenches and trap doors, he made it possible for Jon Berg to reach the models at all times

Matte painting of Hoth and its moons, Mike Pangrazio

1

while they were being filmed. It was on these miniature sets that Jon Berg worked closely with all members of his department. They had to make the eighteen inch and four and a half feet tall models look like fifty feet tall attack vehicles that move with sinister grace. The miniatures later matched the full scale section of the walker built in England around which the live action was shot.

Inspired by the challenge, these artists continued their collaborative effort until the desired effects were completed for the film.

1
Production painting,
Ralph McQuarrie;
Joe Johnston, in collaboration with Ralph McQuarrie, designed the ultrasensory, investigating probe robot which drifts over the surface of Hoth. Like an arachnid, it has long leglike extensions that can reach down and pick up things from the ground as well as draw things in close to its body. The legs are constantly touching ground and pushing off and gesture in a way which makes the Probot appear to be alive. The lenses, like eyes, are also sensing devices. The Probot is armed with laser weapons and can not only defend itself but will self destruct to protect the information that it has gathered. When it is confronted by Chewie, the Probot acts like a gunfighter and whips around to shoot.

The arctic landscape was inspired by pictures of an ice field which had broken up in the spring and had then frozen over. The yellowish sky is similar to the color sometimes seen in arctic regions.
2
Probot emerging from pod,
Norman Reynolds

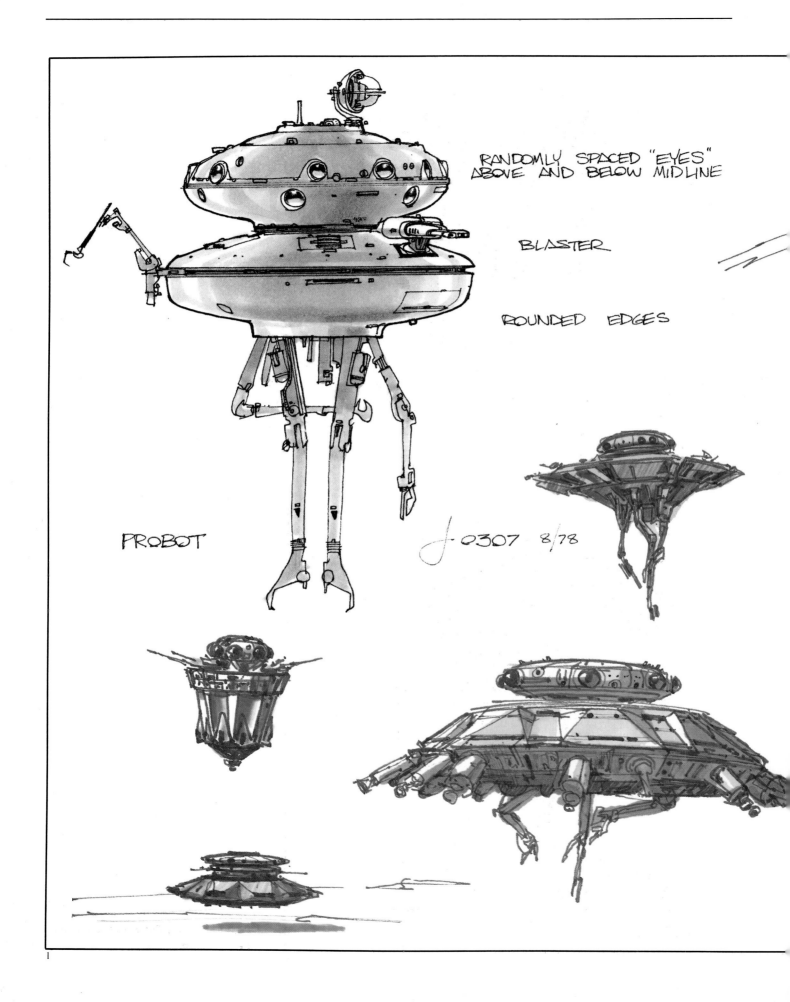

RANDOMLY SPACED "EYES"
ABOVE AND BELOW MIDLINE

BLASTER

ROUNDED EDGES

PROBOT

0307 8/78

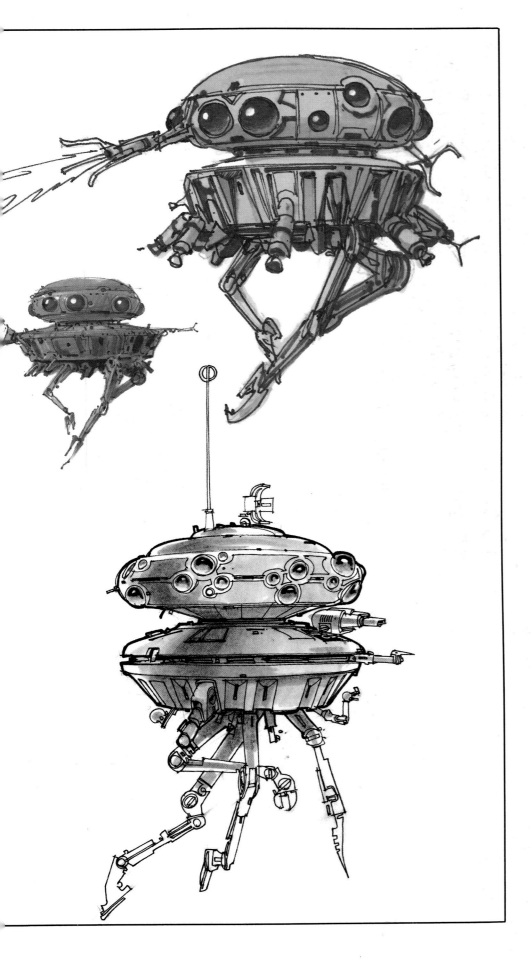

1
Probot sketches, Ralph McQuarrie and Joe Johnston

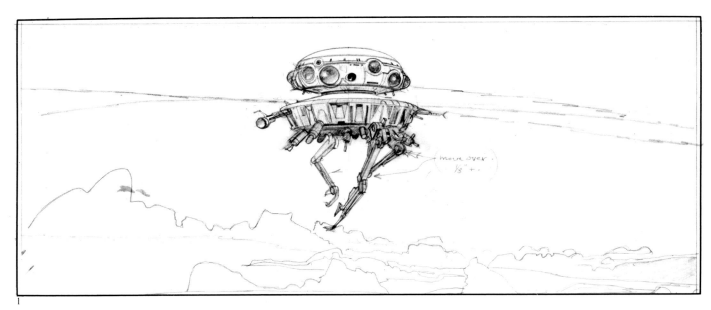

1

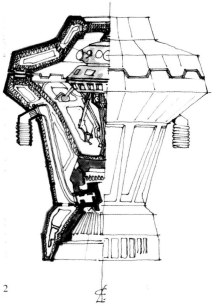

2

1
Sketch for production painting,
Ralph McQuarrie
2
Probot pod sketch, Norman Reynolds
3
Photograph of Probot, George Whitear
4
Preliminary Probot design,
Alan Tomkins under the direction
of Norman Reynolds
1 ▶
Hoth background painting,
Mike Pangrazio
2 ▶
Photograph of Mike Pangrazio by
Howard Stein
3-5 ▶
Hoth background paintings,
Mike Pangrazio

3

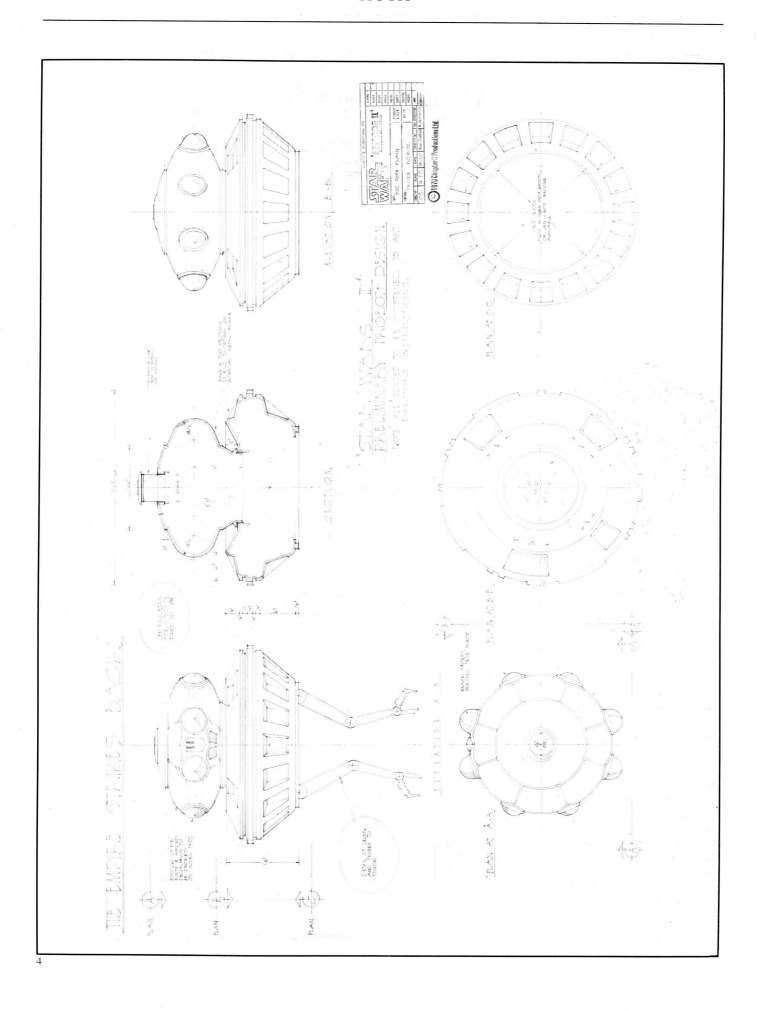

2

3

4

5

1

2

1
Production painting,
Ralph McQuarrie;
*Luke and the Tauntaun have just ridden
to a ridge when the low, moaning growl
of a Wampa Ice Creature captures their
attention. In this conception the Tauntaun is similar to a beast of burden. It
has the ears and nose of a camel, horns
of a yak or other mountain animal and
the rest is kangaroo or dinosaurlike. It
has long fur around the neck and soft
down around its belly. Tauntauns are
an integral part of the life of Hoth.*

*The general effect of this illustration
was to be somewhat reminiscent of an
old-time western hero and his trusty,
beloved horse.*

2
*Preliminary sketches for Tauntaun,
Phil Tippett*

1

2

3

4

5

6

1-2
Preliminary drawings for Tauntaun,
Joe Johnston
3-7
Preliminary drawings,
Ralph McQuarrie

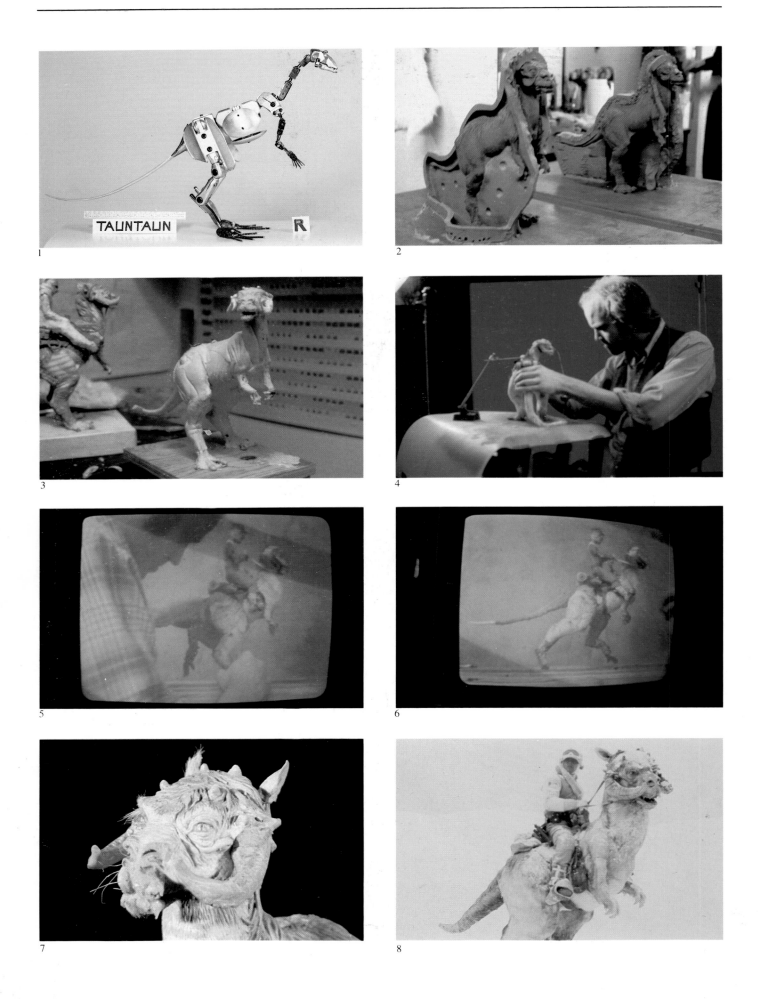

9

1
Mechanical skeleton of Tauntaun,
Phil Tippett
2
Clay model of Tauntaun in mold,
Phil Tippett; photograph by
Miki Herman
3
Clay model of Tauntaun, Phil Tippett;
photograph by Howard Stein
4
Phil Tippett working with Tauntaun
stop motion puppet, photograph by
Howard Stein
5, 6
Tauntaun video tests
7
Head of Tauntaun miniature,
Phil Tippett; photograph by Don Dow
8
Luke on Tauntaun, photograph by
George Whitear
9
Full scale Tauntaun, designed and con-
structed by Norman Reynolds and
Stuart Freeborn

1

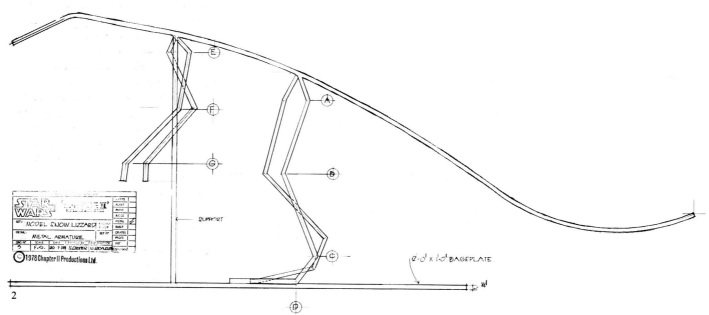

2

1
Production painting,
Ralph McQuarrie;
McQuarrie chose a canyon as the set-ting when he was asked to illustrate the Imperial walkers chasing Luke on his Tauntaun. In this painting, Luke has just ridden up a ravine on his Tauntaun and, surprised by the walkers, he turns to run for his life. In this painting, the Tauntaun's sleek, muscular legs enable it to leap like a deer when confronted by the walker's laser blasts. During this stage of development, the Tauntaun was thought of as being dinosaurlike and potentially vicious yet still willing to obey commands.

The Imperial walkers in this painting represent an early concept and are based on the drawings of Joe Johnston.

2
Metal armature diagram of early Tauntaun, Steve Cooper under the direction of Norman Reynolds

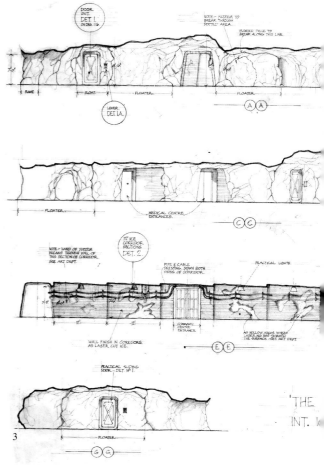

1

2

3

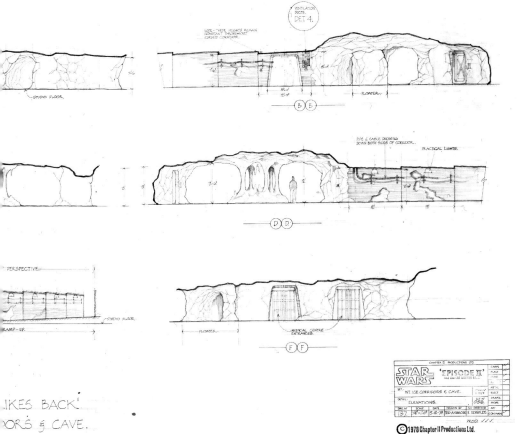

1
Production painting,
Ralph McQuarrie;
The entrance to the Rebel hangar is
hidden from view by a great slab of
fallen glacial ice. McQuarrie studied
many ice formations and glaciers be-
fore doing the painting. For dramatic
composition, he painted the frozen
cliffs in the background a cold blue to
create contrast with the white ice.

The revolving Rebel turret is operated
by people inside. The soldier on top
acts as a tank gunner and his weapon
is close for fighting. A Tauntaun
and rider, probably Han, are shown
for scale.
2
Sketch of Rebel laser cannon turret,
Joe Johnston
3
Elevation of ice corridor,
Ted Ambrose under the direction
of Norman Reynolds

1

2

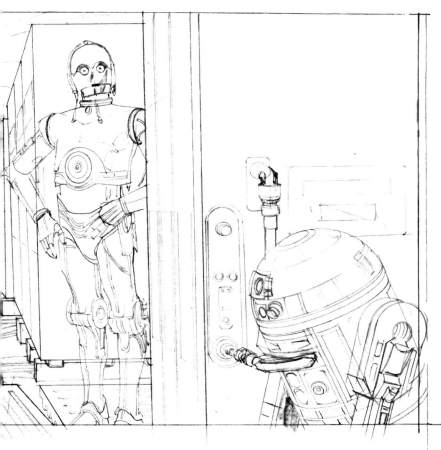

1
Production painting,
Ralph McQuarrie;
The nerve center of the Rebel base is
hidden inside the honeycomb network
of the ice cave complex. Temporary
and portable field equipment has been
brought in by the soldiers manning the
radar consoles. Daylight filters through
the cracks in the ceiling of the tunnel.
The tunnels were probably formed nat-
urally. Powerpacks line the walls
opposite the constantly alert Rebels.
The floor is covered with vacuum-
formed duckboards and is similar to the
covering used on the airfields and
muddy areas during World War II.

See-Threepio and Artoo-Detoo, not
present in many of the production
paintings, were included in this
painting.
2
Sketch for production painting,
Ralph McQuarrie

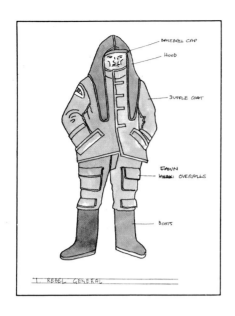

Baseball Cap
Hood
Duffle Coat
Fawn Khaki Overalls
Boots

1 REBEL GENERAL

Cloth Helmet
Khaki Quilted Jacket
Khaki Fawn Overalls
Boots

1 CONTROLLERS ETC

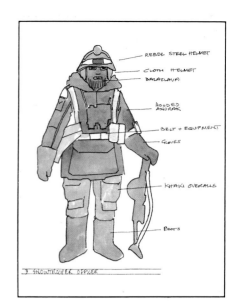

Rebel Steel Helmet
Cloth Helmet
Balaclava
Hooded Anorak
Belt + Equipment
Gloves
Khaki Overalls
Boots

3 SNOWTROOPER OFFICER

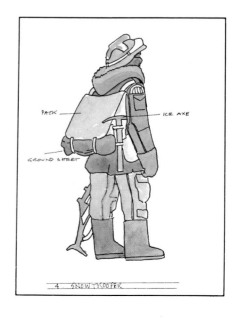

Pack
Ice Axe
Ground Sheet

4 SNOWTROOPER

BASEBALL CAP — CLOTH HELMET

HOODED ANORAK

GLOVES

FAWN OVERALLS

BOOTS

GROUND CREWMAN

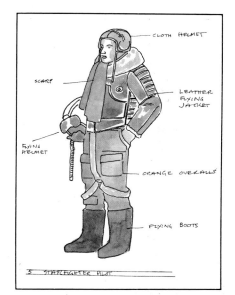

CLOTH HELMET

SCARF

LEATHER FLYING JACKET

FLYING HELMET

ORANGE OVERALLS

FLYING BOOTS

5. STARFIGHTER PILOT

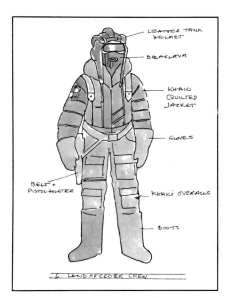

LEATHER TANK HELMET

BALACLAVA

KHAKI QUILTED JACKET

GLOVES

BELT + PISTOL HOLSTER

KHAKI OVERALLS

BOOTS

6. LANDSPEEDER CREW

STEEL HELMET

CLOTH HELMET

KHAKI QUILTED JACKET

CREAM COMBAT WAISTCOAT

GLOVES

KHAKI OVERALLS

8. STAR CRUISER CREW

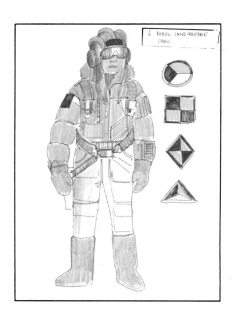

6 REBEL LANDSPEEDER CREW

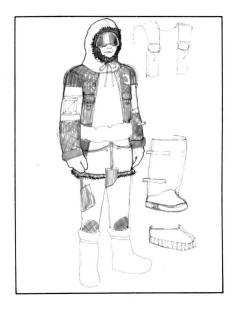

Costume sketches, John Mollo

1

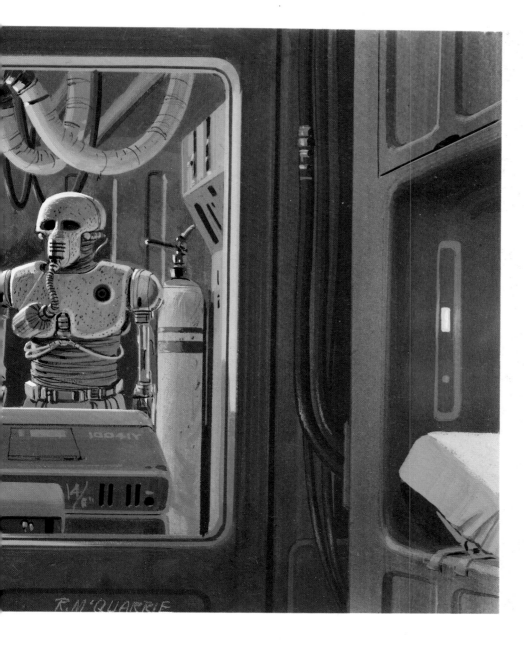

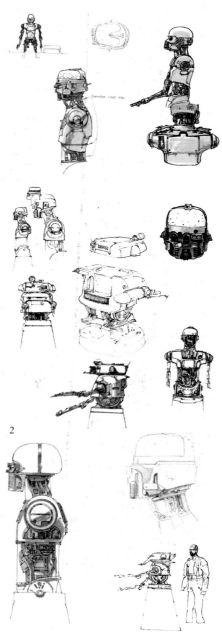

1
Production painting,
Ralph McQuarrie;
After Luke's overnight exposure to
Hoth's fierce environment he is placed
in a bacta tank. Han and Leia await
their friend's rejuvenation from an
adjoining room. The medical staff is
headed by Too-Onebee, a medical droid
with a human brain. The ultimately
logical surgeon, its mechanical support
system is backed up with a micro-
processing computer.
2
Thumbnail sketches of Too-Onebee,
Ralph McQuarrie

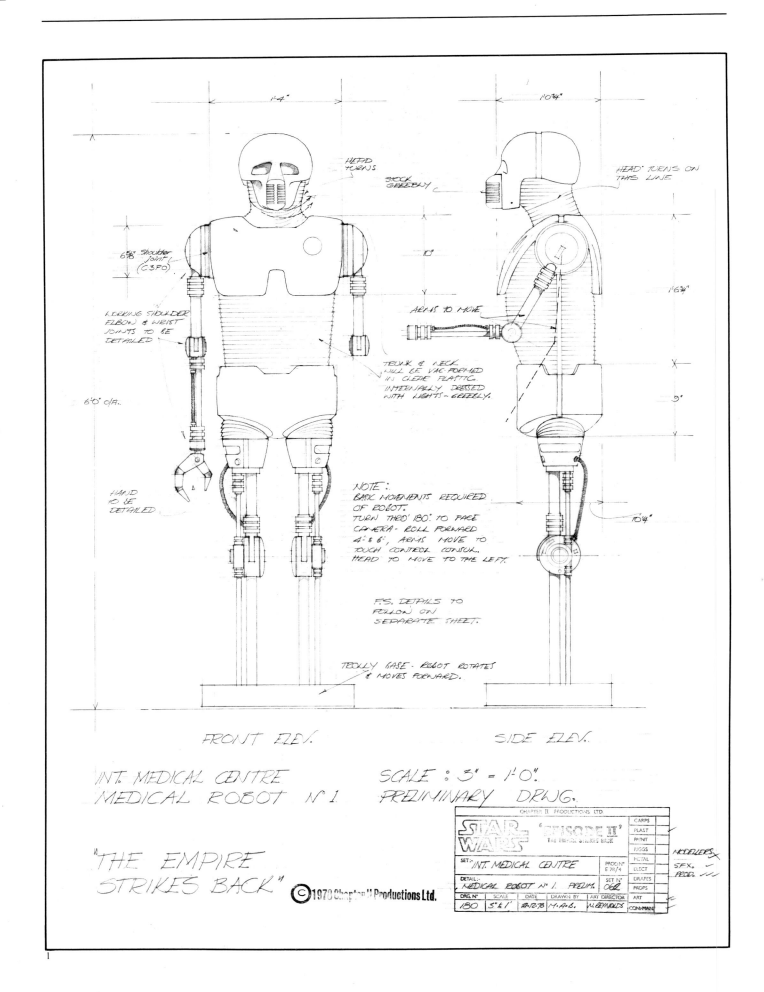

FRONT ELEV.   SIDE ELEV.

INT. MEDICAL CENTRE   SCALE : 3" = 1'0".
MEDICAL ROBOT N° 1   PRELIMINARY DRWG.

"THE EMPIRE
STRIKES BACK"   © 1978 Chapter II Productions Ltd.

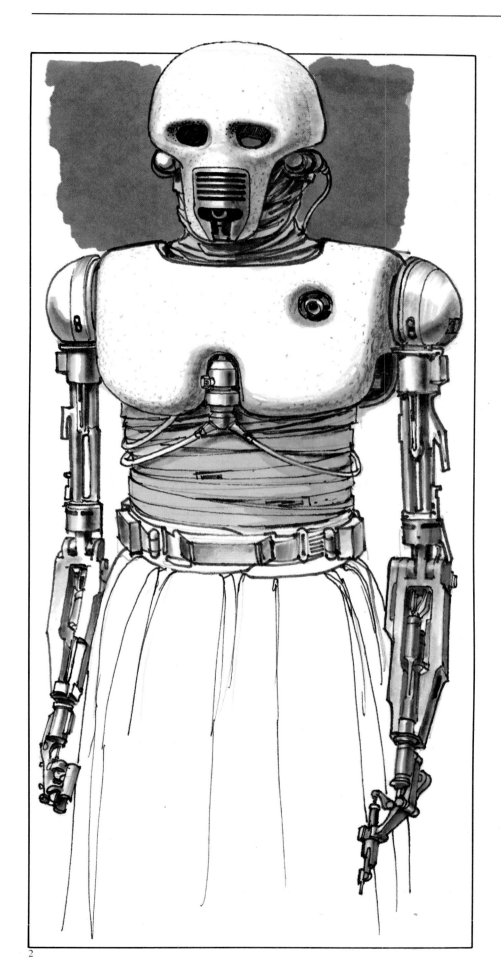

1
Preliminary drawing of Too-Onebee,
Michael Boone under the direction of
Norman Reynolds
2
Sketch of Too-Onebee,
Ralph McQuarrie

2

1

2

4

1

Production painting,
Ralph McQuarrie;
The battle for control of the Rebel generator was fought by troops on foot. At
an early stage in story development, it
was planned that the generator would
be a matte painting and, therefore, it
was placed at the top of the picture to
keep it separate from the live action
plate.

Joe Johnston and Ralph McQuarrie
both worked on designs for the Imperial stormtroopers. The mask over the
stormtrooper's face has a breathing device to warm the air. Johnston added
the hood that covers the trooper's neck
and also designed the laser rifles. On
the stormtrooper's back is a power pack
with miniaturized equipment, radios,
heaters, and other survival apparatus.
The unit insignia on the helmets is a
graphic design of McQuarrie's.
2
Thumbnail sketches of attack on Rebel
generator, Ralph McQuarrie
3
Stormtrooper costume sketches,
John Mollo
4
Sketch for stormtrooper,
Ralph McQuarrie

3

2

1
*Sketches and thumbnails of Rebel
generator, Ralph McQuarrie*
2
Study of stormtroopers, Joe Johnston

1

2

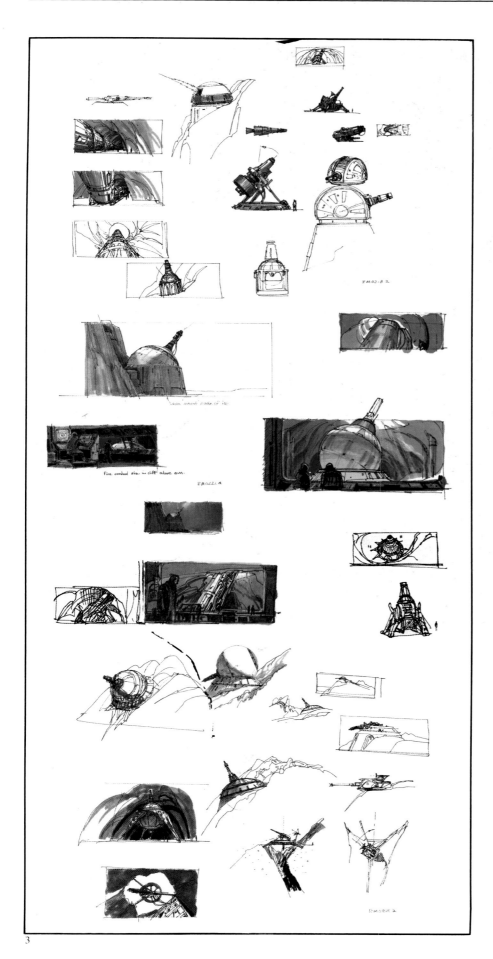

4

1, 2
*Production paintings,
Ralph McQuarrie;*
*While working out the lighting for the
ion cannon control room, McQuarrie
decided to keep the level very low
because the Rebels would be viewing
radar screens. In the process of designing the cannon, McQuarrie began
wondering about the arrangement of
the sighting and control features. It
seemed reasonable to locate them away
from the gun; anything with the power
to destroy a giant spaceship like a Star
Destroyer seemed likely to be dan-
gerous. Putting this room high in the
cliff overlooking the gun seemed logical. The windows can be seen as a
small slot above the gun in the ice cliff.
Seeing the movement of the gun
through the windows would add to the
drama of the scene.*

*The exterior of the ion cannon illustra-
tion was painted as a moonlit scene.*
3
*Thumbnail sketches for ion cannon,
Ralph McQuarrie*
4
Sketch for Rebel, Ralph McQuarrie
1 ▶
*Early construction drawing of ion
cannon, Michael Lamont under the
direction of Norman Reynolds*
2-5 ▶
Stormtrooper costumes, Joe Johnston

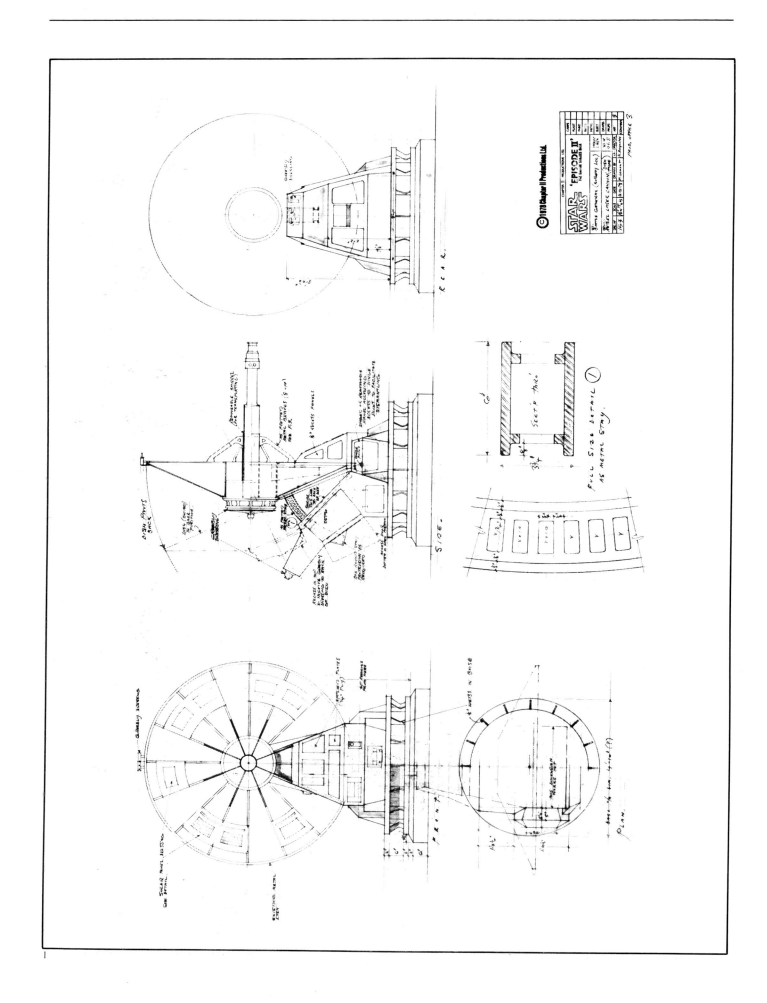

2

3

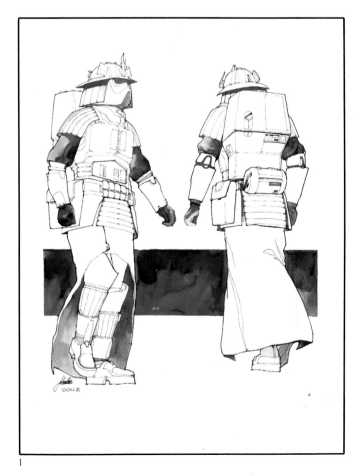

1

5

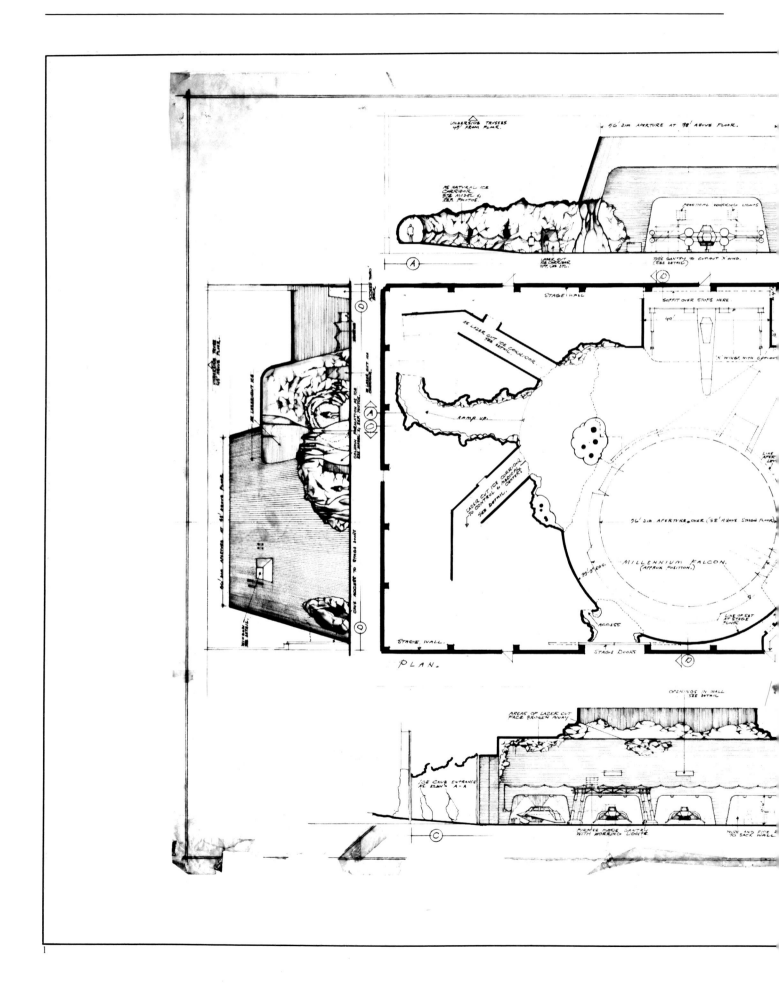

PLAN.

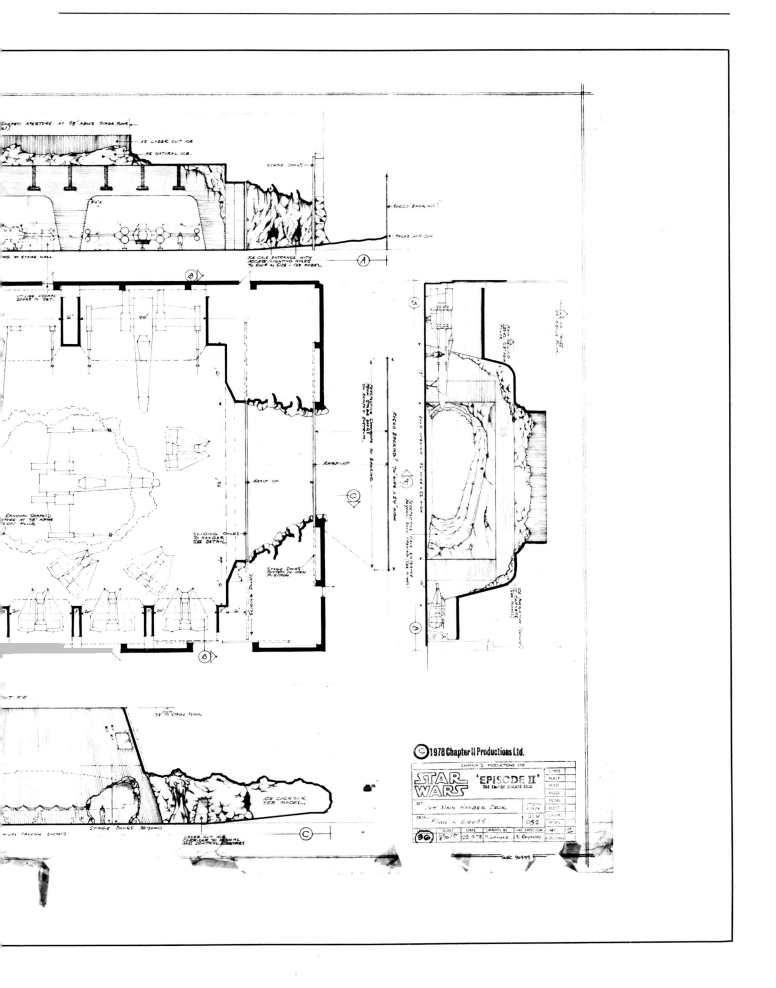

1

2

3

4

1, 7
Sketch for Rebel pilot,
Ralph McQuarrie
2, 3, 4, 6
Production paintings,
Ralph McQuarrie;
These paintings represent the interior
of the ice cave complex. They were
done to indicate where matte paintings
would be needed. Originally McQuar-
rie felt the caves would be filled with
stalagmites or other natural forma-
tions, but it was decided that the Rebels
would have laser blasted the space to
make it larger and more functional.
The serations, caused by the laser
blasting, also made it easy to blend in
matte lines. The matte paintings would
cover up the microphones, lights and
camera cranes which would be on the
live-action plate sent from England
to ILM.

The Rebels devised the complex tunnel
layout so that a direct Imperial attack
could be quickly dispersed.
5
Snowspeeder model, built under the
direction of Lorne Peterson
1 ◀
Stage plan for Rebel hangar,
Michael Lamont under the direction
of Norman Reynolds

5

6

7

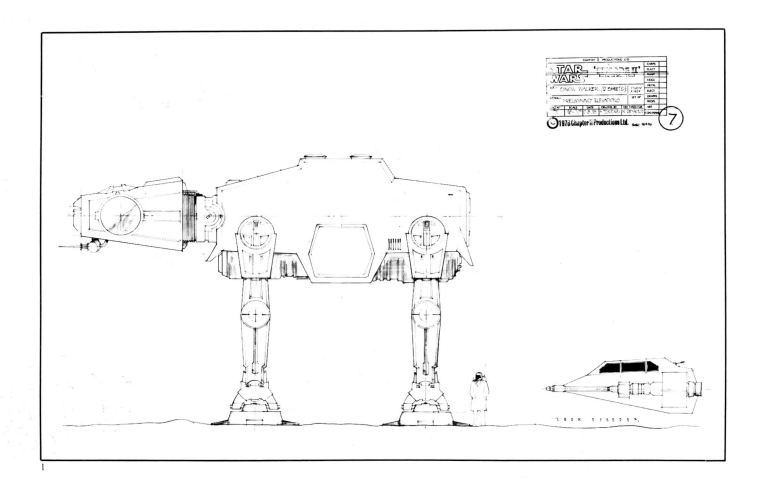

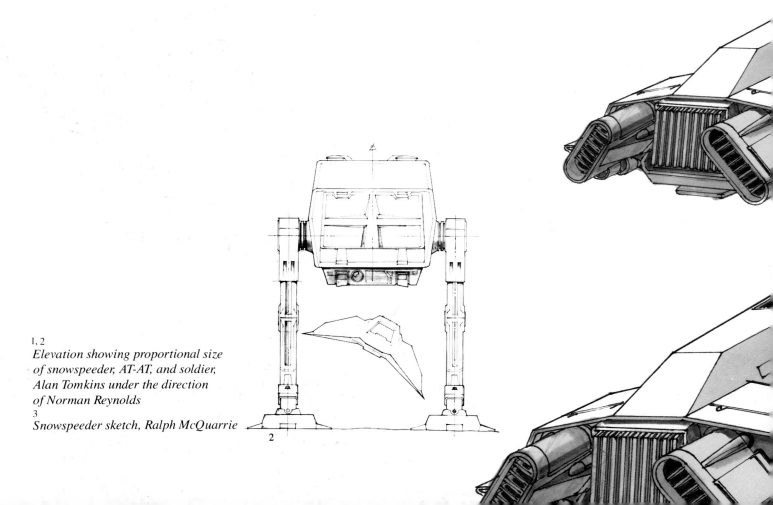

1, 2
*Elevation showing proportional size
of snowspeeder, AT-AT, and soldier,
Alan Tomkins under the direction
of Norman Reynolds*
3
Snowspeeder sketch, Ralph McQuarrie

3

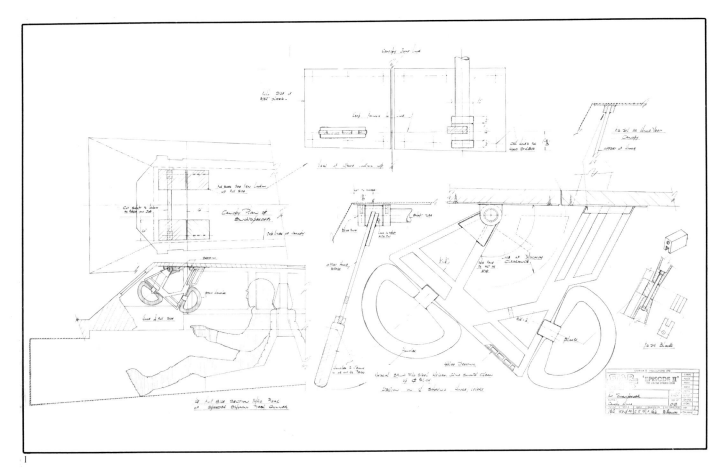

1

1, 2
*Detail construction drawing of
snowspeeder interior and canopy
hinge, Fred Hole under the direction
of Norman Reynolds*
3
*Construction drawing of snowspeeder,
Alan Tomkins under the direction of
Norman Reynolds*
1-4 ▶
*Snowspeeder models, photographs by
Terry Chostner*
5-8 ▶
*Snowspeeder elevations,
Nilo Rodis-Jamero*
9 ▶
*Drawing for camera angle
set-up from interior of snowspeeder,
Michael Lamont under the direction
of Norman Reynolds*
10 ▶
*Sketch to show placement of
pyrotechnic effects, Joe Johnston*
11 ▶
*Construction drawing for gun muzzle,
Fred Hole under the direction of
Norman Reynolds*

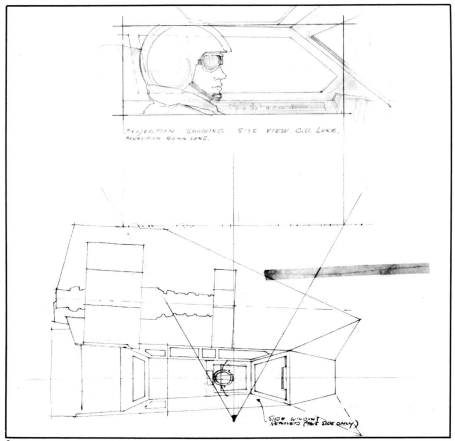

2

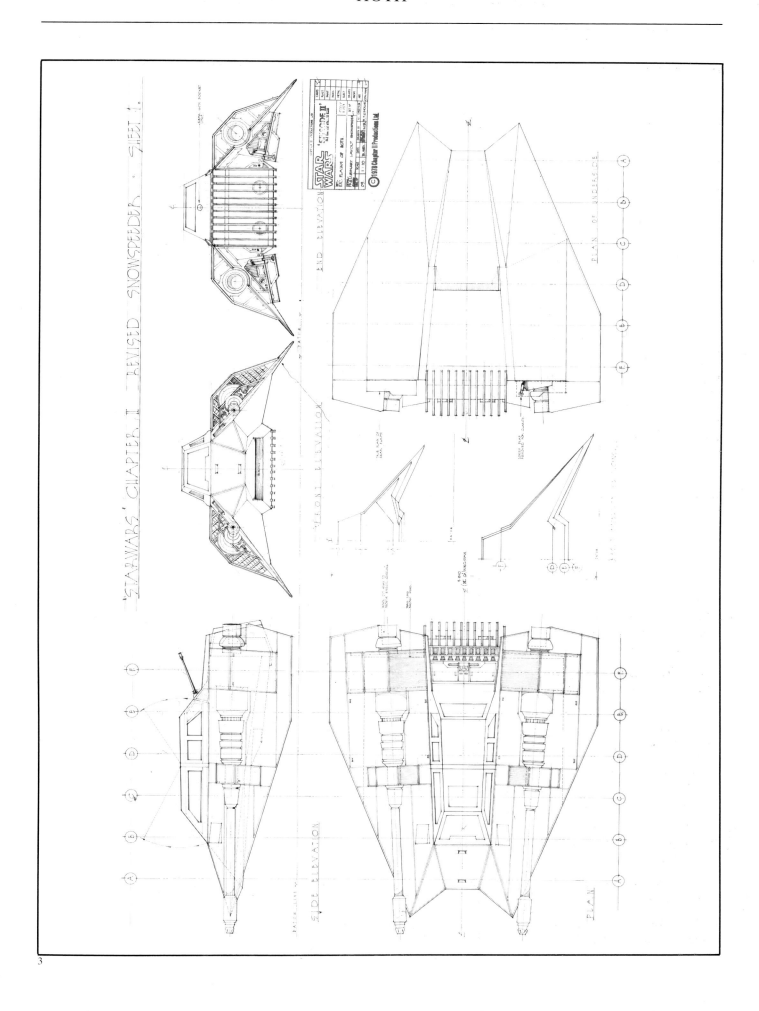

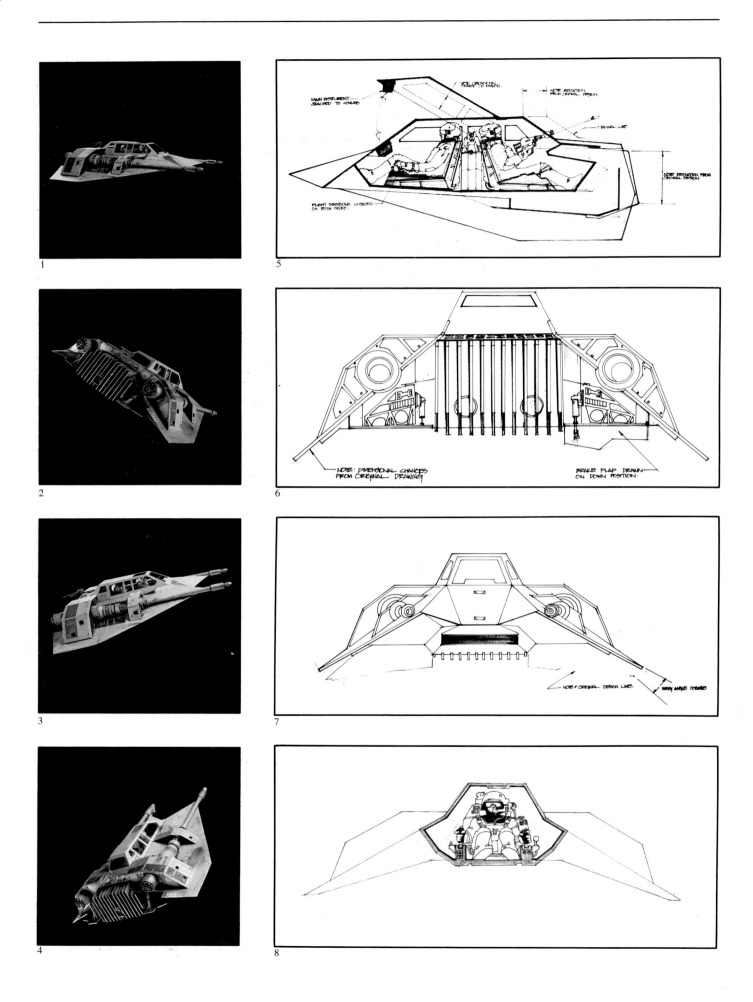

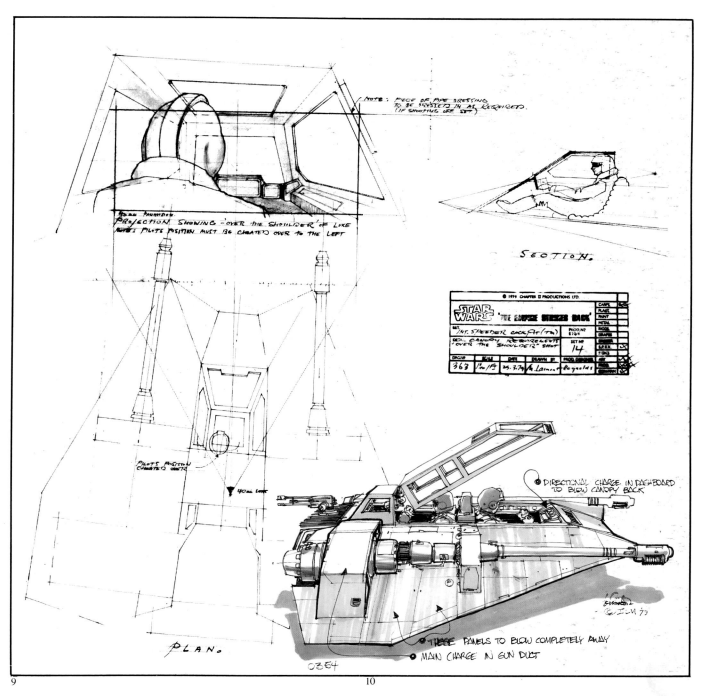

NOTE: PIECE OF PIPE DRESSING
TO BE DRESSED IN AS REQUIRED.
(IF SHOOTING OFF SET)

SECTION.

PLAN PANAVISION.
PROJECTION SHOWING 'OVER THE SHOULDER' OF LUKE
NOTE: PILOTS POSITION MUST BE CHEATED OVER TO THE LEFT

PILOTS POSITION
CHEATED OVER

40mm LENS

PLAN.

0364

STAR WARS 'THE EMPIRE STRIKES BACK'		
SET: INT. SPEEDER COCKPIT (TH)		
DETAIL: CANOPY REQUIREMENTS "OVER THE SHOULDER" SHOT		14
363	1¼"/1'	25.3.79

DIRECTIONAL CHARGE IN DASHBOARD
TO BLOW CANOPY BACK

THESE PANELS TO BLOW COMPLETELY AWAY
MAIN CHARGE IN GUN DUCT

9   10

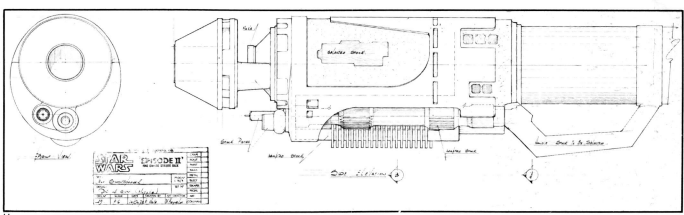

FRONT VIEW.

SIDE ELEVATION

STAR WARS EPISODE II'		

11

1

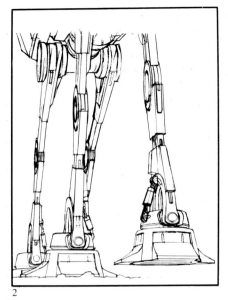

2

3

4

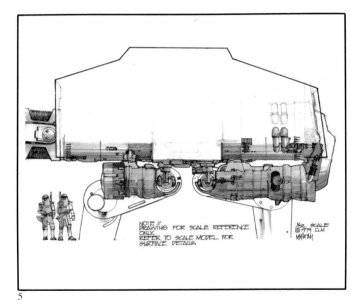

5

6

7

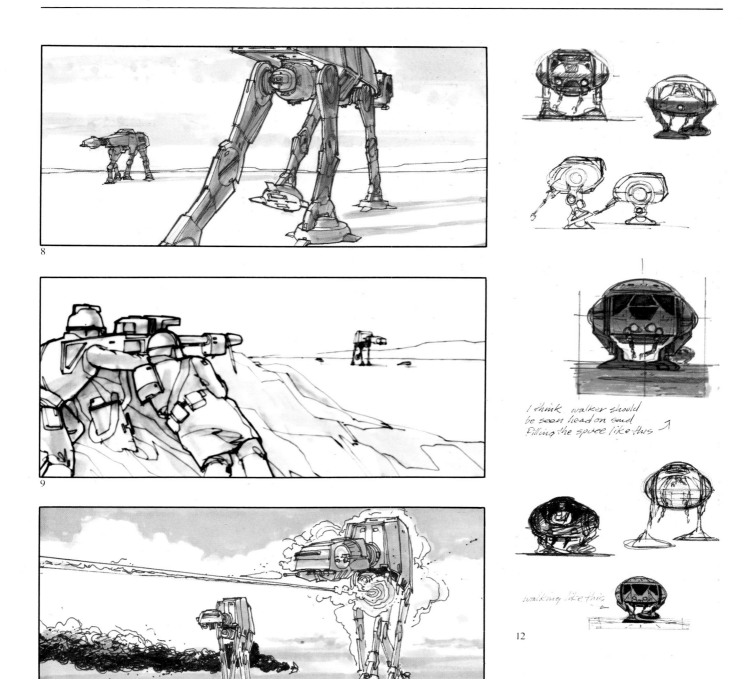

8

9

10

I think walker should
be seen head on and
filling the space like this ↗

walking like this

12

11

1, 3
Sketches for scout walkers,
Joe Johnston
2, 4, 12
Sketches for AT-AT, Ralph McQuarrie
5-11
Sketches for AT-AT, Joe Johnston

1

2

3

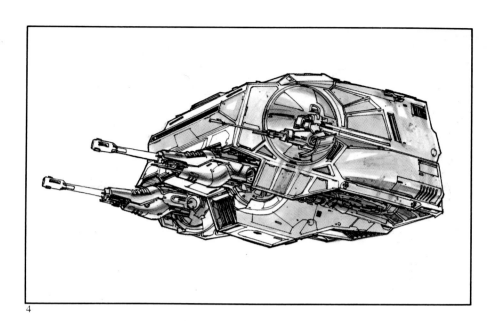

4

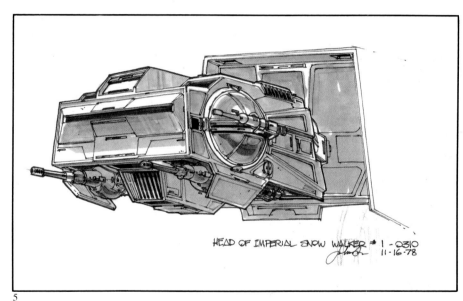

HEAD OF IMPERIAL SNOW WALKER #1 - 0310
11-16-78

5

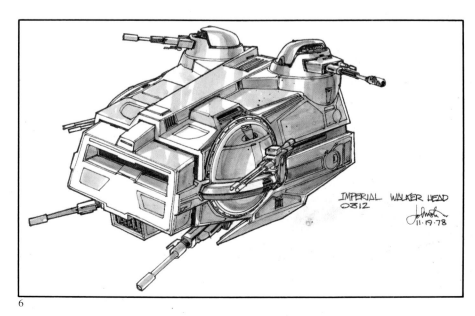

IMPERIAL WALKER HEAD
0312
11-19-78

6

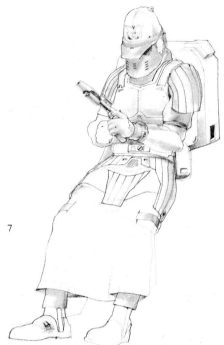

7

1
*Production paintings,
Ralph McQuarrie;
A low-flying Rebel snowspeeder passes
under the nose of a mammoth AT-AT.
The cable attached behind the speeder
is used to lash up the legs of the AT-AT,
bringing the behemoth attack vehicle to
its knees. The flames overhead come
from another speeder which has
been hit.*

*All the speeders are two seaters. The
radar operator doubles as a rear gunner. The pilot faces forward aiming two
heavy laser cannons by pointing the
whole ship at its target, as was done
with the fighter aircraft of World
War II.*
2
*After making several sketches of vari-
ous aspects of the battle, McQuarrie
painted this view of the Rebel snowspeeders circling a crippled walker.
Hit, its front legs have crumbled, knees
first, bringing it down like a large
animal. The cliffs in the background
contain the Rebel stronghold. In the
film, a battle scene like this would be
composed of live action, models and
matte paintings.*
3
*Downed AT-AT model, photograph by
Terry Chostner*
4-6
Sketches for AT-AT head, Joe Johnston
7
*Early sketch of stormtrooper,
Joe Johnston*

1

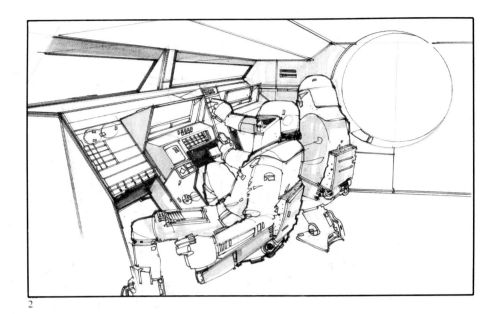

2

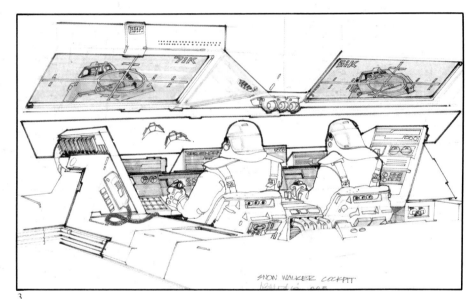

3

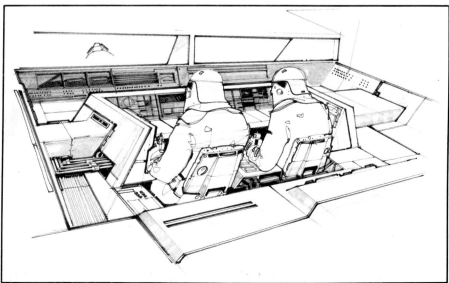

4

1
Thumbnail sketches for Hoth battle sequence, Ralph McQuarrie
2 - 4
Interior of AT-AT head manned by stormtroopers, Nilo Rodis-Jamero
5
Composite photograph of AT-AT models, Terry Chostner
6
AT-AT sketch, Joe Johnston

5

6

1
Production painting,
Ralph McQuarrie;
This is the moment when Luke scram-
bles out of his crashed snowspeeder
and must decide if he's going to run
from the charging AT-ATs before the
smoke clears. Painted to complete
the collection of key action shots,
McQuarrie captures great detail in this
moment: the bent laser cannon, the
gouged furrow of ice and the smoke
and steam resulting from the collision
between the hot metal of the blasted
speeder and the ice. This effect on film
would be a combination of live action,
models and matte paintings.

John Mollo designed the flight suit
and gear.

1
*Photograph of AT-AT's against
background painting, Don Dow;
airbrushing by Ralph McQuarrie
and Bob Jacobs*

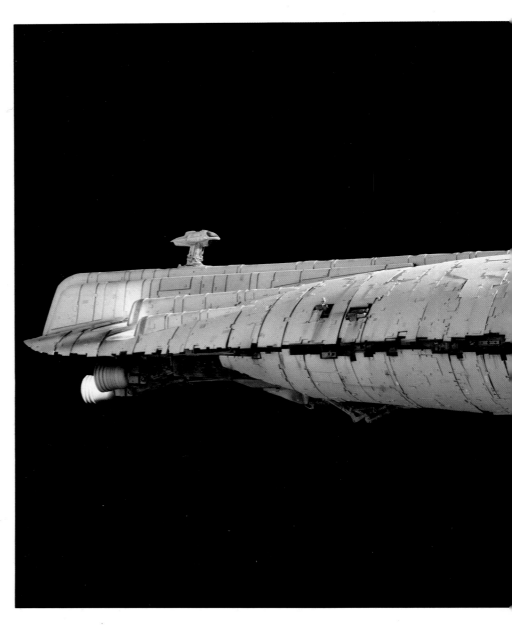

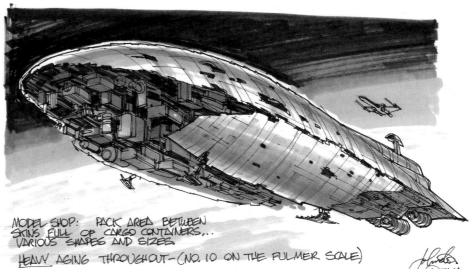

1
Rebel Transport model, built under the direction of Lorne Peterson
2, 3
Sketches of Rebel Transport, Joe Johnston

MODEL SHOP: PACK AREA BETWEEN
SKINS FULL OF CARGO CONTAINERS...
VARIOUS SHAPES AND SIZES

HEAVY AGING THROUGHOUT- (NO. 10 ON THE FULMER SCALE)

0352

2

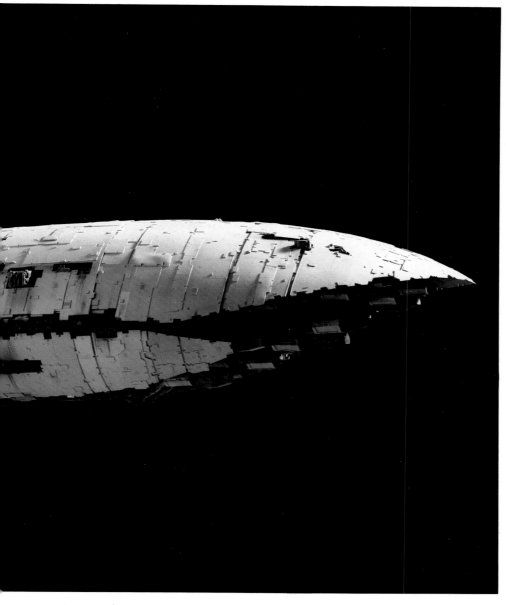

rebel transport in ice hangar / Hoth
© ILM 79
0353

3

1

1
Production painting,
Ralph McQuarrie;
Painted from a still photograph of the
live-action, McQuarrie tried to cap-
ture as many elements of the trench
sequences as possible. He changed the
angle and added an Imperial AT-AT
overrunning a Rebel laser turret as
snowspeeders retreat in the back-
ground.

Facing defeat, the Rebels realize that, if
not taken prisoner, it is unlikely they
will survive a frozen night on Hoth.
2
Elevation of Rebel trenches,
Michael Lamont under the direction
of Norman Reynolds

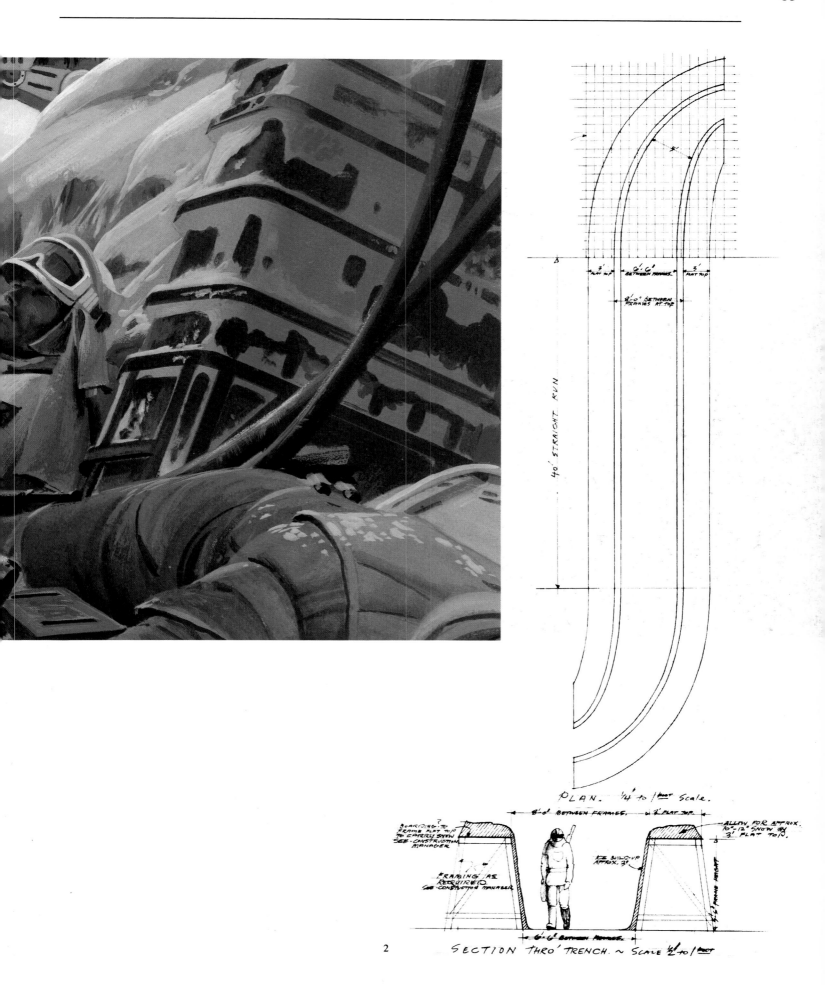

PLAN. ¼ to 1 foot Scale.

SECTION THRO' TRENCH. ~ SCALE ½ to 1 foot

2

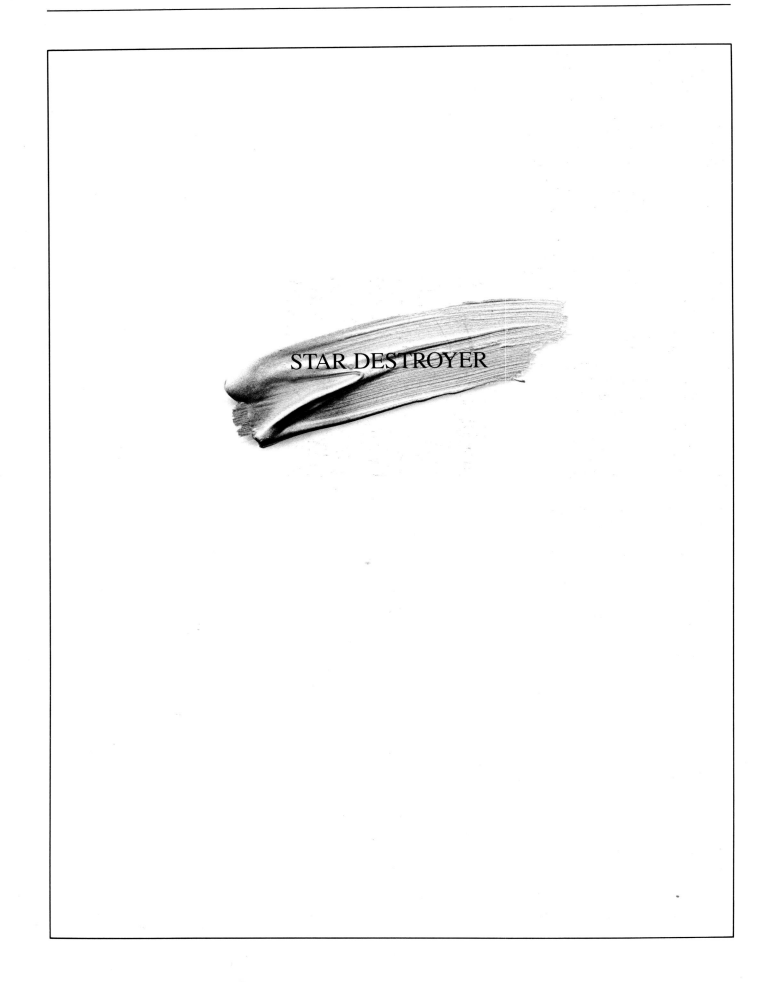

STAR DESTROYER

Led by Darth Vader in his Star Destroyer, the Executor, the Imperial
fleet deploys a horde of AT-AT's to
crush the Rebel encampment on Hoth.

The Executor is the Empire's top of
the line vehicle with twice the destruc-
tive capability of any other craft in the
Imperial fleet. Originally designed for
use in a few establishing shots, Vader's
Destroyer evolved into one of the
film's central locations. Once the ten
foot long model was placed in front of
the camera and seen with its two hundred and fifty thousand lights ablaze,
the storyboards were quickly changed
to make the Executor one of the major
vehicles in THE EMPIRE STRIKES
BACK.

The scenes that take place in the
Executor were filmed basically on
two sets. Designed by Norman
Reynolds, these sets include the control bridge and Darth Vader's private
chamber. The remaining locations on
the Executor were done as matte
paintings. The control bridge set, with
its star-filled panoramic windows,
reflects Vader's unquenchable thirst
for power.

Reminiscent of slave ship galleys,
enlisted men work at the feet of their
superiors. On this set Vader's newest
and most efficient ally, Boba Fett, a
bounty hunter from the Mandalore
system, is introduced. Boba Fett's costume, with wrist lasers, rocket darts,
and flying backpack design, is a collaboration of design efforts of Joe
Johnston and Ralph McQuarrie. Built
at EMI Elstree Studios in England,
this suit of armor was shipped back to
Johnston at ILM so that he could paint
and age it.

Darth Vader's private chamber was
hydraulically functional with the two
halves separating like a huge pair of
hands with interlocking fingers. It is in
this chamber that the Lord of Sith
removes his mask and contemplates
his dark soul. Equipped with a direct
comlink to the Emperor, Vader
remains one of the most powerful
beings in the galaxy.

Star Destroyer model, photograph by
Nancy Moran

1

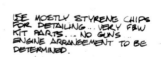

USE MOSTLY STYRENE CHIPS
FOR DETAILING... VERY FEW
KIT PARTS... NO GUNS
ENGINE ARRANGEMENT TO BE
DETERMINED.

©ILM 6·12·79

2

Production painting,
Ralph McQuarrie;
This painting was done as an establishing shot for a promotional trailer
released in European theaters. We see
Hoth as a sphere of ice textured in
shades of blue and white. Painted with
camera movement in mind, there is
great perspective if you focus past the
bottom of the Star Destroyer and onto
Hoth's distant moon.
2
Sketch for Star Destroyer model,
Joe Johnston

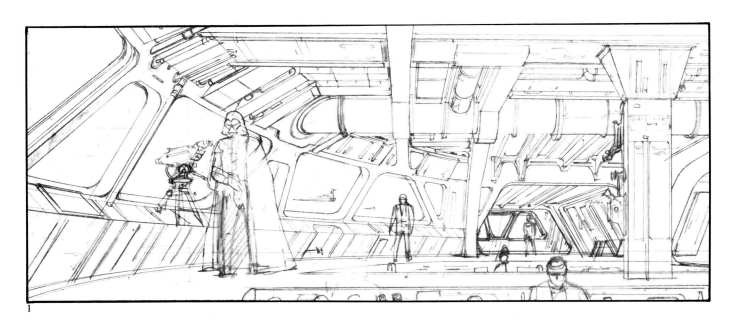

1

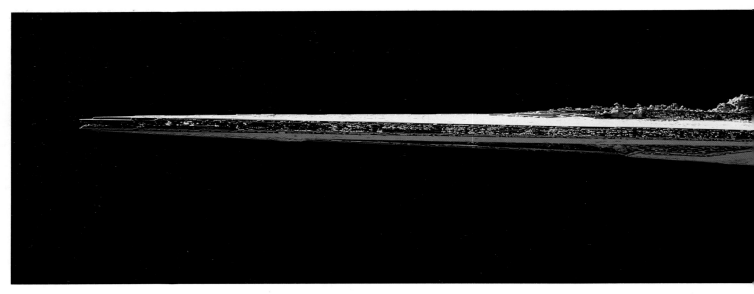

3

1, 2
Sketches of Star Destroyer bridge,
Ralph McQuarrie
3
Photograph of early Star Destroyer
model, Howard Stein
4
Darth Vader sketch, Ralph McQuarrie
1 ▶
Composite photograph of Millennium
Falcon evading the Empire's Star
Destroyer fleet. Models photographed
by Terry Chostner, airbrushing by
Ralph McQuarrie and Ron Larson.

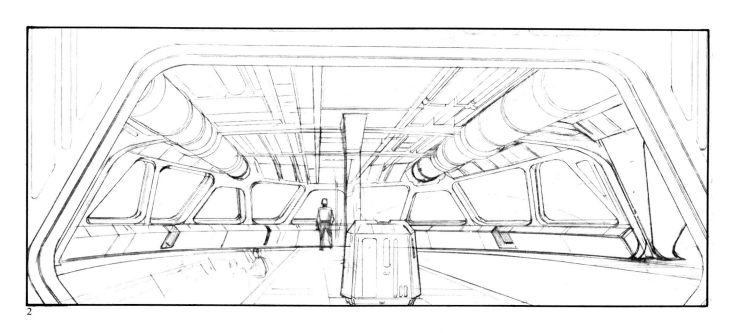

2

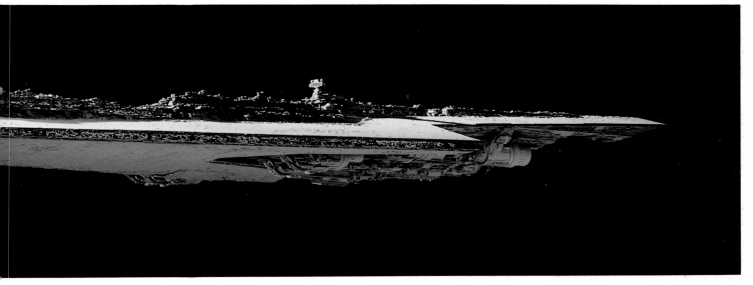

4

1

1

2

1, 4
Sketches of Darth Vader's meditation chamber, Norman Reynolds
2
Production paintings,
Ralph McQuarrie;
Controls for space ships are usually shown within the heart of a vehicle for protection, but the shielding force field of the Star Destroyer allows the ship's control bridge to be at the head of the vehicle. The walkway down which Darth Vader strolls is placed low so that his view is not obstructed. McQuarrie used large windows to make the setting more dramatic and also to allow for panoramic views of planets and other passing ships.
3
A view straight down the nose of Darth Vader's Star Destroyer is similar to the view of a cockpit of a large aircraft. In the center is a console which contains telephones and other equipment. The men at the controls operate equipment connected to various parts of the ship, such as the radar room which is located in the vehicle's interior. Overhead ducts, electronic gear and equipment panels were detailed in matte paintings for the film.

3

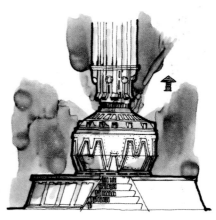

1

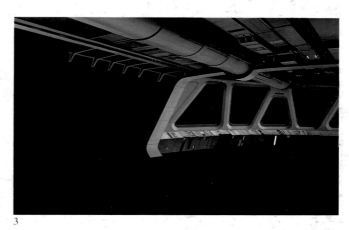

1
Matte painting of Star Destroyer bridge with live-action plate, Ralph McQuarrie

2
Stage set of live-action plate, photograph by George Whitear

3
Matte painting, Ralph McQuarrie

1

3

2

4

5

8

6

7

1-8
Studies and thumbnail sketches of meditation chamber and Emperor, Ralph McQuarrie

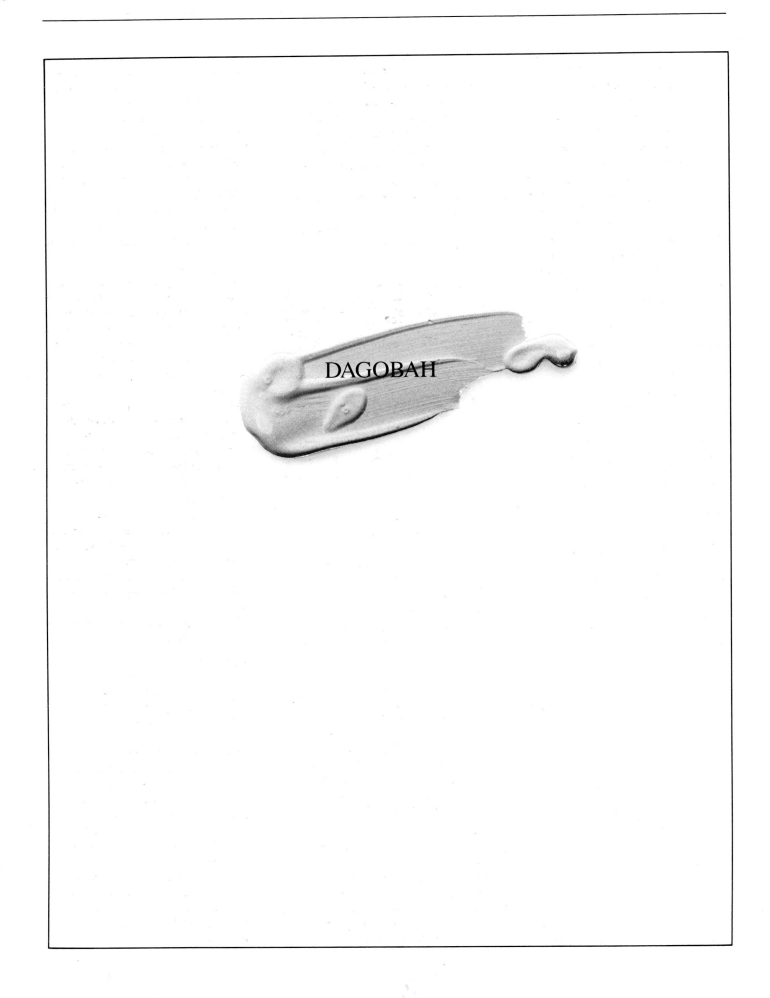

DAGOBAH

Having barely escaped the Imperial AT-AT onslaught back at Rebel base Hoth, Luke finds himself out in deep space with no planned destination. In his mind's eye he sees a strange distant planet and he can hear the echo of Obi-Wan Kenobi telling him to trust his feelings. So, with faith, Luke once more lets the Force guide his ship. His course takes him to Dagobah, a planet that is uncharted on any galactic map. Apprehensive, Luke and his co-pilot, Artoo-Detoo, slowly descend into the atmospheric mist that enshrouds the planet. As they lower their X-wing to the planet's surface they clip the tops of giant swampland trees and crash-land into a miry bog. Frantically they try to salvage their sinking craft, for it is their only means of escape from this fog-ladened world of quagmires and lagoons. During their struggle they are unknowingly observed by Yoda, an eight hundred year old Jedi sage. Out of friendship for Obi-Wan Kenobi Yoda will make sure that no harm befalls the young warrior, and more importantly, it is he who will decide whether Luke is worthy of further spiritual teaching in the ways of the Force.

There was a short moment in time when entrance to this mystical land of make-believe could actually be obtained here on the planet Earth. By a quirk of metaphysical law, between the months of August and October in the year nineteen hundred and seventy-nine, by entering the sound stages at EMI Elstree Studios in England, one could transcend space and imagination to arrive worlds away at Yoda's mystic dwelling place, the bog planet Dagobah.

Lucas wanted Dagobah to be a dark and spooky jungle swamp planet with many hidden secrets. At one point shooting on location in real swamplands was considered. Associate producer Robert Watts searched the swamps of Florida, South America, the Caribbean, and East Africa for locations. The filmmakers finally decided that if an actual swamp was to be used the production factors would be too risky and that the final look would be too earthbound. So, they devised a swamp of their own and inhabited it

with the vermin of their imaginations. Conceptual artist Ralph McQuarrie painted the earliest vision of this ever so eerie environment and picked up on the idea of giant banyan trees, which are common in swamps throughout the world. These massive trees have exposed root systems which grasp onto the eroded soil. It was thought that the exposed roots of the trees on Dagobah would be petrified in grotesque forked and gnarled shapes after millenniums of standing bare to the

elements. Once an overall design direction for Dagobah was agreed upon, it became production designer Norman Reynolds' responsibility to create this primitive world so that it could be filmed.

Like the working situation in California, those involved in the design in England worked on many worlds at once. Hoth might be on one stage while Bespin was being built on another. A typical day for Reynolds would begin with checking the progress of the work done on all of the soundstages and making whatever alterations were needed. Some of the construction was beginning on one set, some half-way through and some finishing. At one point, he was scrambling to finish six or seven sets at once.

Reynolds' first major task was to create the trees for the Dagobah forest. Although he found inspiration in McQuarrie's paintings, he decided to base his trees on those which are found in the swamps of Nigeria. He began the trees with tubular steel skeletons,

then shaped them by using wire mesh and textured them with plaster. This is similar to the process a student would use in constructing a volcano for a science fair, only this project was on a slightly larger scale. The trees stood forty feet high and were up to ten feet in circumference. Each tree was approached as a separate set unto itself. As the designer, Reynolds gave careful thought as to how the individual trees would have been affected by the elements over a long period of time.

The lagoon was to be a three foot deep, wooden pool. Because the stage floor was concrete, the pool could not be dug into the ground. This meant that the entire playing area of Dagobah had to be raised on platforms at least three feet high. The raised platforms facilitated the building of the rolling terrain, the lagoon and also made it easier to hide Yoda's operators. The use of platforms allowed Reynolds a certain amount of flexibility; the sections of the stage could be moved, thus increasing the number of variations in backgrounds and locales.

For the scene when Luke is seen climbing out of the X-wing cockpit and onto the crashed vehicle's wing, a full scale replica of the ship was constructed. When the ship was finished, it weighed thirty tons and had a magnificent forty foot wing span. The X-wing was then placed in the lagoon where it appeared partially submerged in the quagmire.

Reynolds' crew of two hundred skilled technicians and laborers worked day and night to keep construction up with the shooting schedule. Elstree Studio had been used to house all of the sets and Dagobah was the last to go up. Even as the dreaded deadline approached, things could not be rushed to the point of compromising the effect. Prop people were sent out to scour the countryside in a twenty mile radius around the studio for turf and vines to dress the set. They sent back truckload after truckload of vines locally known as "old man's beard." These can be seen draped throughout the jungle. Thousands of pieces of turf

Matte painting of Dagobah, Mike Pangrazio

1

1

were turned upside down to create the marshy ground. Once the set was dressed with all the vegetation it came to life. Even the film equipment scattered around its perimeters, cameras on cranes, overhanging cables for microphones and the huge arc lights all looked quite grand. When it was finished the total set filled an area approximately the size of two and a half football fields. Though not a Guinness Book recordbreaker, it was one of the world's largest soundstage sets.

This eerie environment became Yoda's home. Lucas wanted Yoda to be nonhuman yet have the characteristics of an intelligent, wise old sage. He was to be the epitome of an important

mind with a calm soul. Joe Johnston drew sketches of Yoda as a wrinkled, gnomish-looking dwarf with withered hands and odd feet for tromping in the mud. Ralph McQuarrie made him less cute-looking with high pronounced cheek bones and a prominent bridge on his nose. These conceptualizations were taken to make-up artist Stuart Freeborn who sculpted the working model and gave Yoda his final character. Basically, within the skull is a very complicated mechanism that can move the eyes from side to side, up and down and around. The eyelids can be opened and closed. The ears can be twisted and moved up and down. Articulation in the mouth and teeth and

tongue can be coordinated. Yoda also has the ability to furrow his brow and make numerous other facial expressions. Frank Oz is primarily responsible for bringing Yoda to life with the assistance of Kathryn Mullen and Wendy Midener. Among them they carefully orchestrate all of Yoda's movements with their hands and fingers.

A hermit like his Jedi brother, Obi-Wan Kenobi, Yoda is an environmentalist. He is at one with the nature of the universe. It was thought that his house would have a rounded dome and be mosque- or church-like. His house is a temple of environmental efficiency, made of mud, sticks, stones

impossible to operate Yoda mechanically a complete radio controlled version was used.

One of the film's more serene segments, it is from Yoda that Luke learns to control his youthful anger and begins to understand the passive strength of the Force.

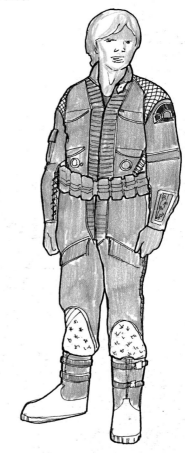

and other naturally existing material found on Dagobah. His windows are transparent gems. Norman Reynolds found it best to use treated styrofoam, paint and stained glass to achieve this required effect.

It was important that the interior of the house represent Yoda's character. So, Reynolds placed it by a lagoon because he felt Yoda would appreciate the falling rain. Yoda would not use technical appliances. Everything, including his furniture and storage spaces, had to seem handcrafted by Yoda. Even the scrolls that hang on the walls looked as though they were in his own hand.

Miniature clay models of the set and characters were used to figure out lighting and camera angles in Yoda's small hut. Also, it was important to know what movements puppet master Frank Oz and actor Mark Hamill would have to re-create for the storyline. Such a limited space, with so many various components, does not lend itself well to improvisation.

Frank Oz manipulated Yoda by sticking him on his arm and walking about. A channel had to be cut and the floor had to be removable in various places. Oz and his assistants would operate from a hole in the floor in situations where Yoda did not actually walk about. In those situations where it was

1
Production painting,
Ralph McQuarrie;
Luke frantically tries to salvage his sinking X-wing in this early concept of Dagobah's environment. Dagobah is a bog planet; the whole effect was to be dark and eerie. McQuarrie painted tangled undergrowth and giant banyan trees in this first interpretation of the swamp. At a later stage the banyan trees were considered too earthlike but the idea of trees with exposed root systems was retained. The use of fog seemed an obvious way to lend atmosphere and realism to the swamp set.
2
Sketch of Luke, John Mollo
1 ◄
Matte painting of Dagobah's surface and cloud cover, Mike Pangrazio

1

2

3

4

BOG PLANET - STARWARS STAGE   PLAN SCALE

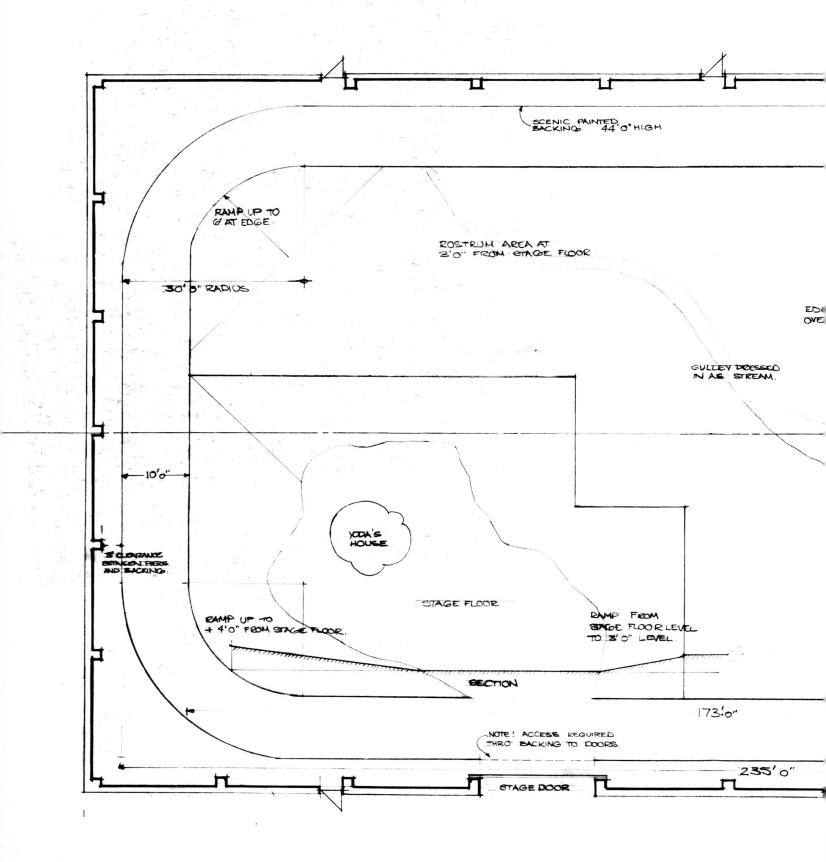

SCENIC PAINTED
BACKING 44'0" HIGH

RAMP UP TO
Ø AT EDGE

ROSTRUM AREA AT
3'0" FROM STAGE FLOOR

30'0" RADIUS

EDG
OVE

GULLEY DRESSED
IN AS STREAM.

10'0"

YODA'S
HOUSE

3" CLEARANCE
BETWEEN PIERS
AND BACKING.

STAGE FLOOR

RAMP UP TO
+ 4'0" FROM STAGE FLOOR.

RAMP FROM
STAGE FLOOR LEVEL
TO 3'0" LEVEL

SECTION

173'0"

NOTE! ACCESS REQUIRED
THRO' BACKING TO DOORS

235'0"

STAGE DOOR

0"

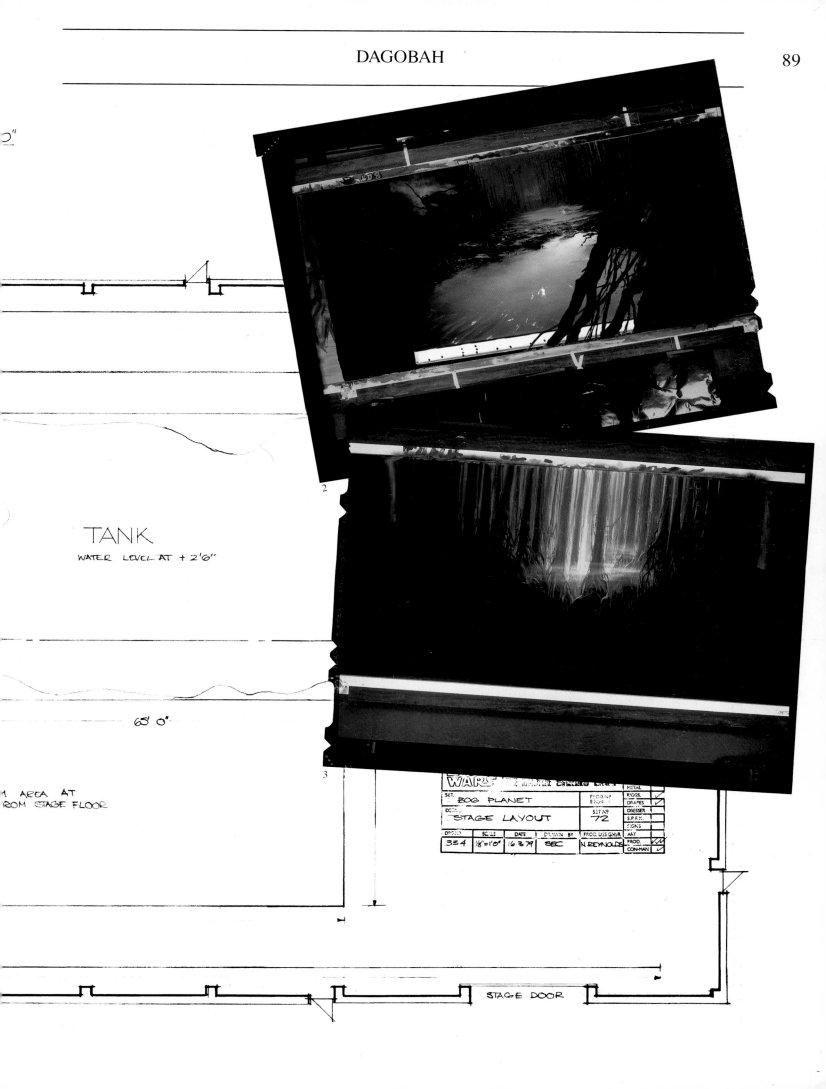

TANK

WATER LEVEL AT + 2'6"

65' 0"

2

3

...M AREA AT
...ROM STAGE FLOOR

WARS				METAL	
SET. BOG PLANET			PROD N° E3794	RIGGS.	✓
				DRAPES	
DETAIL STAGE LAYOUT			SET N° 72	DRESSER	
				S.P.FX.	
				SIGNS	
DRG N° 334	SCALE 1/8"=1'0"	DATE 16.3.79	DRAWN BY SBC	PROD DESIGNER N REYNOLDS	ART
					FROD. ✓✓
					CON-MAN ✓

STAGE DOOR

1
Sketch of Yoda, Joe Johnston
2, 4
Head studies for Yoda,
Ralph McQuarrie
3
Head studies, Joe Johnston

1

2

3

4

1

2

3

4

5

6

7

8

9

10

1-8, 10
*Developmental sketches of Yoda,
Joe Johnston*
9
Yoda sketch, Ralph McQuarrie

1

1
Production painting,
Ralph McQuarrie;
Yoda made his house out of mud and
clay. Since light from Dagobah's sun
rarely breaks through the cloud cover-
ing and thick forest, there is a hearth in
each room for warmth. Skylights and
windows filled with precious stones let
in what little light there is.

1

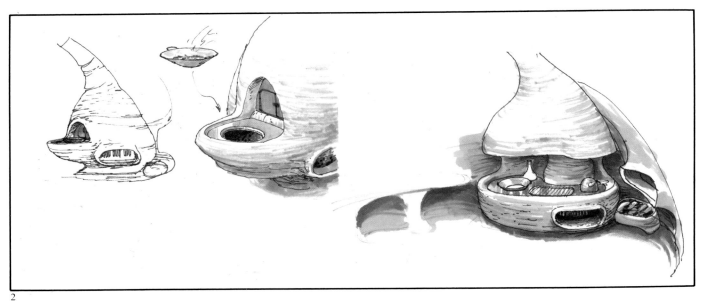

2

1
Sketch of Yoda's house in swamp forest,
Ralph McQuarrie
2, 3
Sketches for house interior,
Ralph McQuarrie

3

4

5

6

4
*Production painting,
Ralph McQuarrie;
Living in a constant state of twilight,
Yoda spends most of his time in meditation studying ancient documents and
diagrams. The cabinet on the wall rep-
resents one of the most technically
advanced objects in the house and
holds some of Yoda's private posses-
sions. The bottle suspended from the
ceiling holds either water or wine.*

5
*Sketch for production painting,
Ralph McQuarrie*

6
*Sketches of planet vegetation,
Ralph McQuarrie*

1

2

3

1
Yoda's house and surrounding swamp,
photograph by Murray Close
2
Artoo-Detoo peeking into Yoda's house,
by Murray Close
3
Photograph of Yoda
by George Whitear

1

2

3

1
*Production painting,
Ralph McQuarrie;
The air is muggy and dank as a shirt-
less Luke carries Yoda on his back. The
tree roots resemble claws or spider
legs. Covering the ground is a field of
paludial fungi with embryonic mem-
branes. A sticky, white fluid is secreted
by these "yogurt" plants. With Yoda as
his guide, Luke travels through this environment on his transcendental jour-
ney of growth.*
2
*Thumbnail sketches for mystic tree
interior, Ralph McQuarrie*
3
*Sketch of Luke entering mystic tree,
Ralph McQuarrie*

1

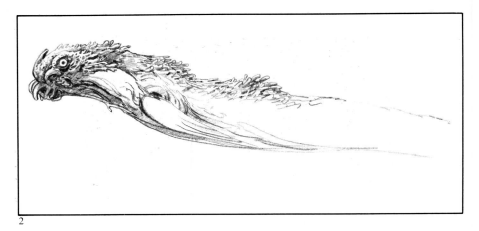

2

3

4

5

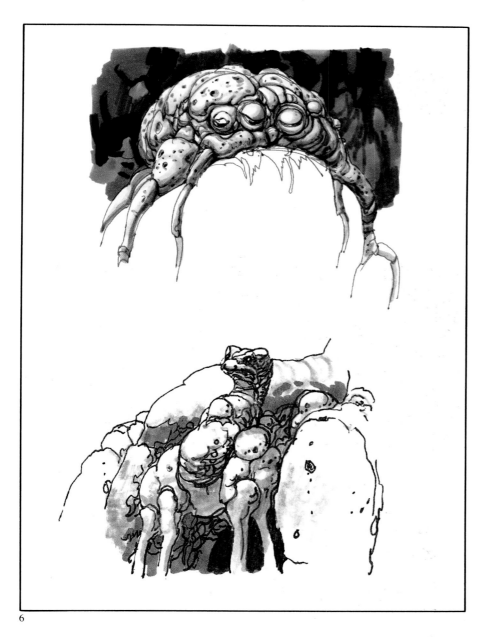

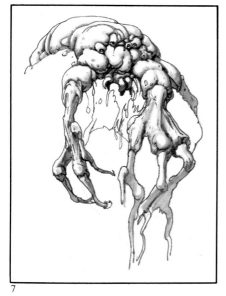

1-8
Swamp creature sketches,
Ralph McQuarrie

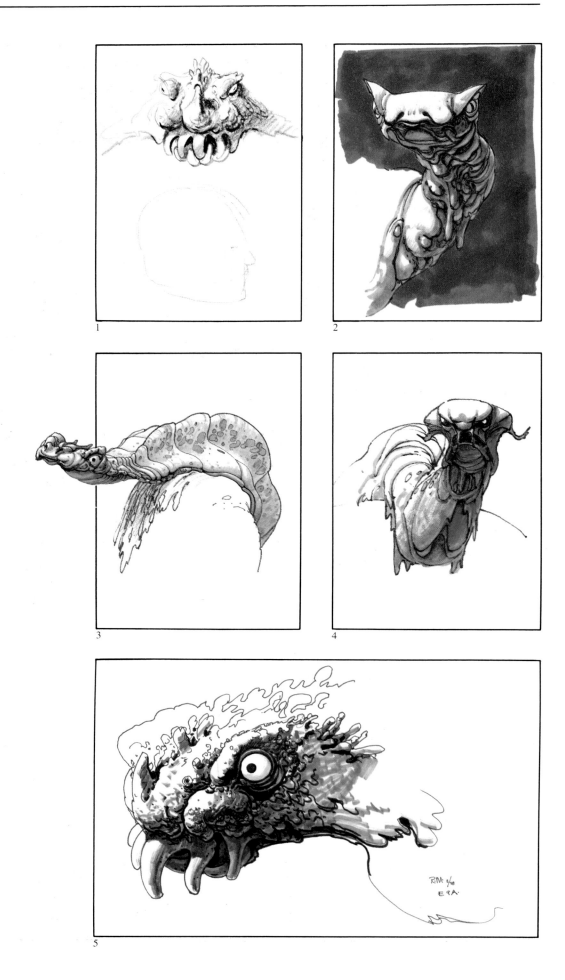

1-6
Swamp creature sketches,
Ralph McQuarrie

1

1
Production painting,
Ralph McQuarrie;
Though the scene is pictured differently
in the film, McQuarrie's painting more
than captures the feeling of Luke's de-
parture from Dagobah. The young
Rebel solemnly vows to his teachers
that he will continue his reflections into
the ways of the Jedi Knights.

ASTEROID BELT

Unable to get the Millennium Falcon in to hyperdrive, Han Solo decides to try his luck at outmaneuvering the attacking Imperial TIE fighters by passing through a turbulent asteroid belt.

The fast paced asteroid sequence is the cumulative work of many special effects artists combined with the work of the ILM optical department headed by Bruce Nicholson. Though the whole sequence lasts under two minutes, its construction was very complex and consisted of as many as twenty-five separate photographic elements. The asteroid sequence required extensive visual overlapping of these elements and would not have been possible without the use of an optical printer. An optical printer is a duplicating machine which is made up of several projectors and a camera. All are mounted so that the projected images can be rephotographed by the camera. This allows flexibility in changing the direction and speed of an image or in repositioning an image in a frame.

Gliding along the ridges and caverns of a large asteroid, Han ducks the Millennium Falcon into a cave and plans to wait until the Imperial forces have left the area.

The Millennium Falcon model used in the first film was four feet in diameter and weighed over one hundred pounds. This model was too heavy to use in order to make the intricate maneuvers in the asteroid sequences seem believable. A lighter, thirty pound model was constructed that could flip, twist and turn on a computerized support. A full scale Millennium Falcon, eighty feet in diameter and weighing twenty-three tons, was constructed in a shipyard in Wales for the live-action photography in England. It was built in sixteen sections for easy transport and storage and will also be used in several other STAR WARS films.

The Rebels' stay is cut short when they discover that what they have flown into is not really a cave but the mouth of a giant space slug. Though we only see the slug for a few frames, Nilo Rodis-Jamero paid special

attention to designing the right texture and scale for the model.

The animation department was headed by Peter Kuran. One responsibility of the department involved the effects of sparks and flashing lights that occur as the TIE fighters and asteroids collide during the chase of the Falcon through the asteroid belt. The animated sparks and lights were airbrushed and backlit then matched frame by frame with the models, asteroids and the starfield. This department also created cartoon

animated storyboards called animatics. While editing the live action sequences, the film editors used the animated storyboards to fill in special effects sequences which were to be added later. The animatics helped the editors to more easily envision the film in total, and were also useful in coordinating the pacing and timing of the effects shots.

Stunningly visual, the whole sequence is a prime example of the necessity to heighten reality when dealing with fantasy.

Composite shot of Millennium Falcon evading TIE fighters; Terry Chostner, airbrushing by Bob Jacobs and Ron Larson

1

2

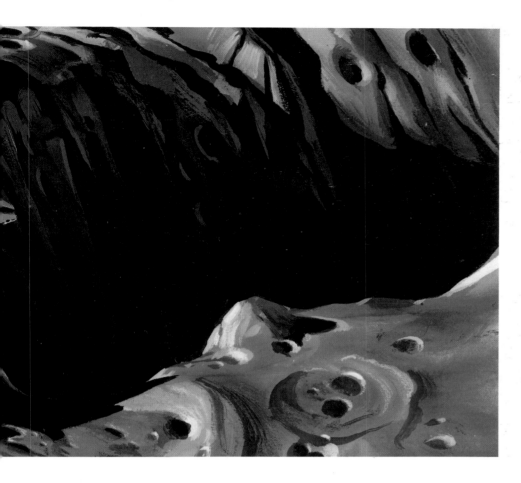

1
Production paintings,
Ralph McQuarrie;
The flaring explosions in this painting occur as asteroids collide in their movement through space. In the film excitement was added by having Han dodge through the narrow canyons and craters of an even larger asteroid. In his efforts to escape the ongoing asteroid storm, he discovers this cave.
2
After coming to rest in what they believe to be merely a great cave, the Rebels are startled to find the floor of the cave moving and the entrance growing smaller. They leap to the controls and fly through what turns out to be a gap in the teeth of a huge creature.

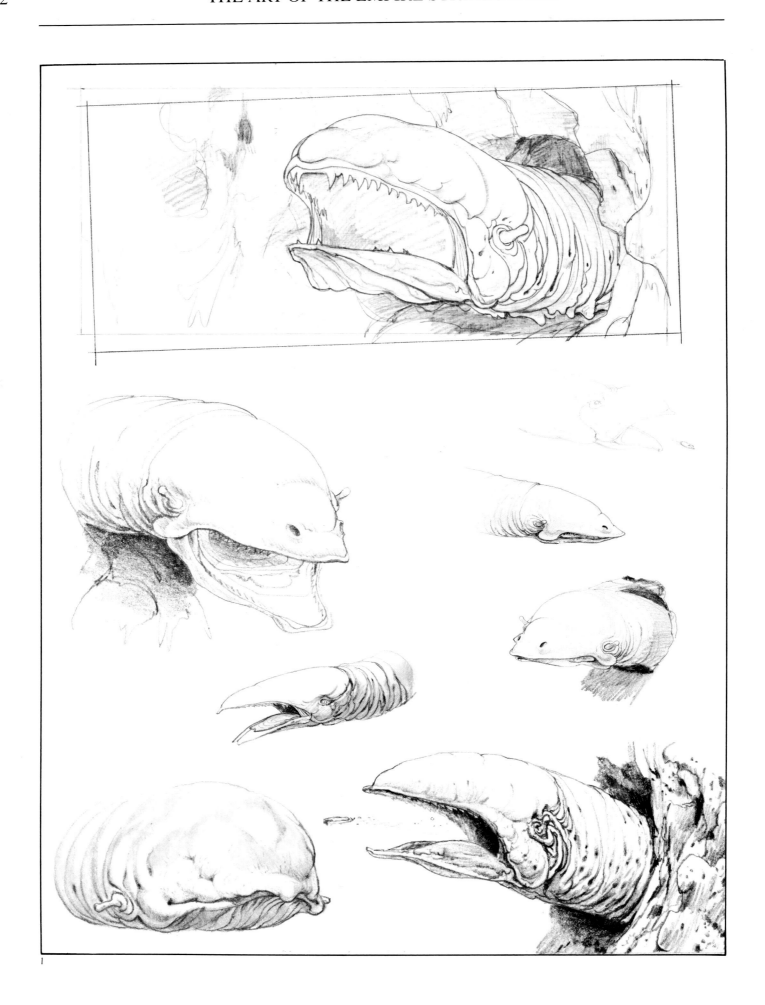

1
Sketches for space slug,
Ralph McQuarrie
2
Sketches for Mynocks,
Ralph McQuarrie

2

1

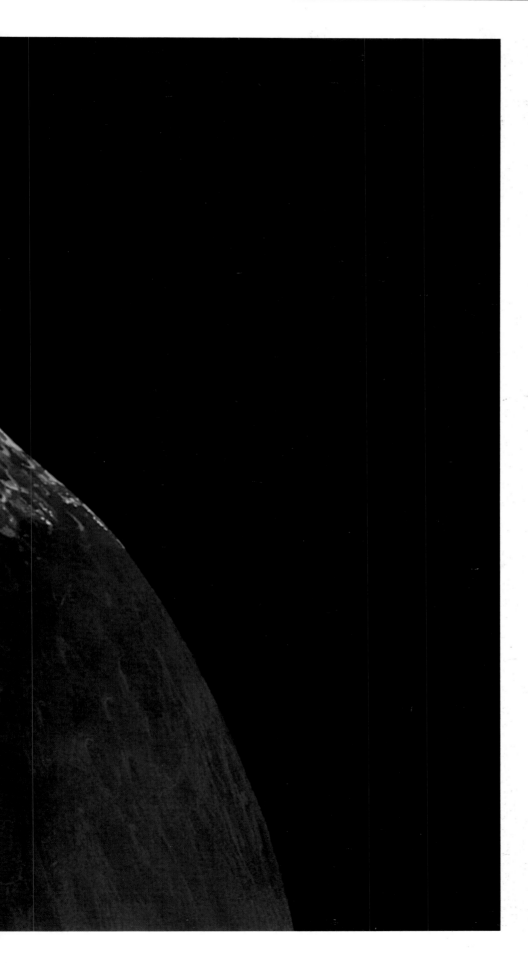

1
Matte painting of asteroid surface,
Mike Pangrazio

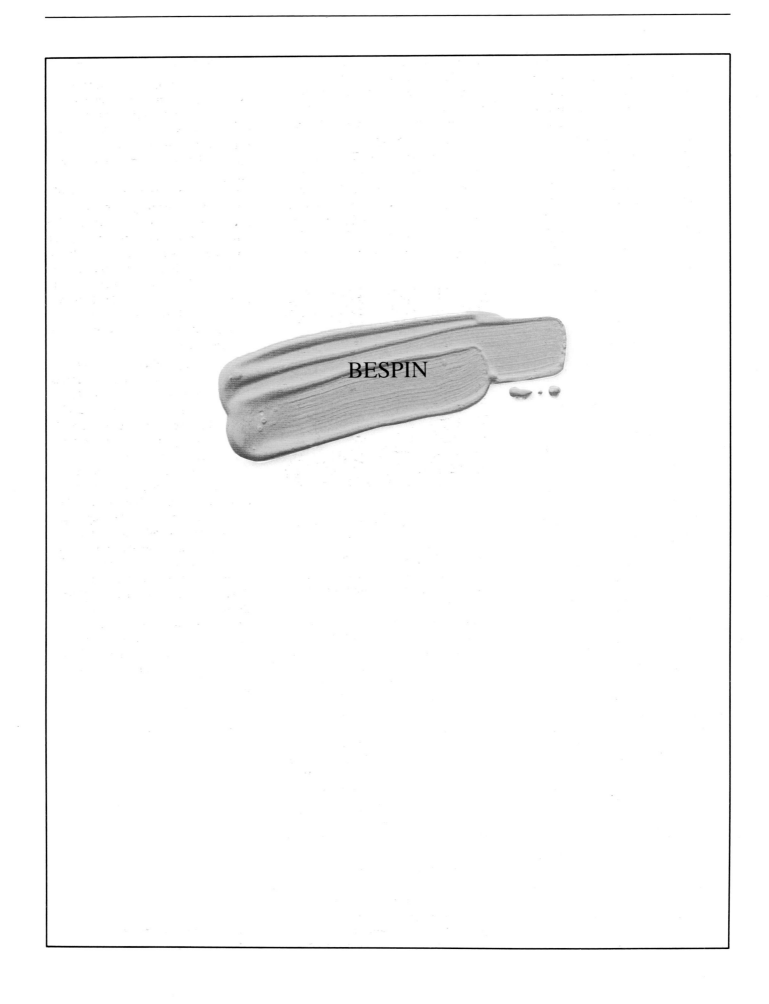

BESPIN

Bespin's wondrous Cloud City is one of the galaxy's major trading ports. It floats above the planet and rests upon a shaft which leads to a huge processing generator. Cloud City citizens are an industrious people whose advanced technology enables them to export the rare anti-gravitational tibanna gas. Governed by flamboyant, ex-soldier of fortune and former owner of the Millennium Falcon, Lando Calrissian, Cloud City remains a neutral colony. Han Solo retreats to the center of this bustling free market to harbor the malfunctioning Millennium Falcon. Han hopes that his old running partner, Lando, will provide sanctuary for Princess Leia and Chewbacca.

Ethereal as a painter's brush stroke, the concept of a floating city was first thought of as a possibility for an Imperial prison city in STAR WARS. This part of the story disappeared in a script rewrite but George Lucas liked the image very much so the floating city was held onto for use in THE EMPIRE STRIKES BACK.

It was difficult to make the scenes that take place in Cloud City believable. This difficulty was heightened by the fact that the viewing audience would know that such a location does not exist. Subconsciously they would register the fact that some trick had to be used. The challenge for the art department and the matte painters was to create a new world without disrupting the story's believability.

In THE EMPIRE STRIKES BACK, the Cloud City of Bespin has a circular, streamlined quality. This look predominates the city's architecture and vehicles. Extending this motif to the city's interior spaces, production designer Norman Reynolds wanted the reactor shaft sets to show the vertical, tubular structures that support the surface shapes. In the carbon-freezing chamber, Reynolds opened up the structures forming geometrical patterns. This theatrical setting became the stage for Luke's climactic duel against Darth Vader. Built twelve feet off the ground, the set allowed the camera to be positioned at dramatic angles for Han Solo's frozen interment and Luke's vengeful lightsaber duel.

The matte painting department at ILM is headed by veteran matte artist, Harrison Ellenshaw. Responsible for over eighty separate paintings in THE EMPIRE STRIKES BACK, Ellenshaw was assisted by design consultant, Ralph McQuarrie and Mike Pangrazio. This department was instrumental in the careful planning of the paintings. The desired effect was charted out in storyboards and the painters were responsible for keeping up with changes in location, character, and

composition of each particular shot.

A matte painting is, very simply, a painting done to blend with the photographic elements of a shot to make the final result look completely real. During this process the matte painter must communicate closely with the production designer since the paintings must convey the style of the sets. The most common technique used for matte painting is to have the subject matter painted on a piece of glass and have the live action projected onto a clear area. The two primary methods of projection used are front and rear. This technique can be best illustrated by using a scene from THE EMPIRE STRIKES BACK as an example: Han has just landed at the Cloud City landing platform and is greeted by Lando Calrissian. The actors appear in the live-action plate which was shot in England. The matte painting depicts the city's skyline at sunset. The live action is then projected onto a reflective screen which is the skyline painting. The combined image is then bounced back at a camera and

refilmed to make a final negative.

When a front projection process is used, the live-action plate cannot be moved. It must be refilmed in the exact frame position it had when originally shot. If the images don't match up the painting must be redone. The rear projection process allows for a little more freedom. Because of differences in the projector, the live-action plate can be reduced and repositioned to fit into the matte painting. The live action is projected from behind the painting onto a translucent material. The scene in which Princess Leia looks out over Cloud City from Lando's penthouse suite is a perfect example of the use of the rear projection technique.

When matte paintings are combined with live action and miniature effects in a front projection process called latent imaging, a different process is involved. Several exposures are made. One is developed while the others are kept in refrigeration. The developed film is examined to make sure the matte painting is aligned through the entire sequence. If all goes well, then the second exposure is developed and given to the animation department. This shot with the matte paintings and animation creates the final image. The other exposures, as a safety precaution, are stored for future use. When the film gets to the matte painting phase, the filmmaker realizes the potential of the live-action footage. It then becomes the task and challenge of the matte painter to make this potential a reality.

Matte painting of Bespin,
Mike Pangrazio

1

1
Production painting,
Ralph McQuarrie;
Buoyed above the clouds, this majestic city is bathed in golden sunlight. Once the headquarters of great leaders, the city's various levels represent all strata of society from the lowest mining Ugnaught to the highest royal official. Having grown at random, evidence of the city's glorious past is seen in the monumental structures which remain. The top level is reminiscent of the New York City skyline. The verandas along the sides are actually huge landing ports.

Joe Johnston designed the twin-pod cloud car, seen on the left amidst the dust clouds.

1

2

3

5

6

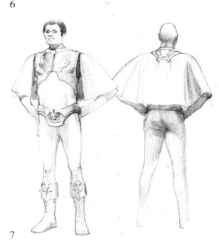

7

1-3, 7
Lando costume sketches,
Ralph McQuarrie
4
Production paintings,
Ralph McQuarrie;
A full scale replica of the Millennium
Falcon was built for scenes such as the
Rebels' escape from Cloud City. The
structure created many new angles from
which the cameraman could film the
live action. McQuarrie's production
painting was done as a matte study of
the city's towers and horizon.
5
Illuminated by northern lights, the
landing platform is located up in the
towers atop Cloud City. When the Mil-
lennium Falcon arrives, Han and Leia
are met by Lando and his aide. At the
time McQuarrie was doing this paint-
ing the character of the aide was not
yet developed and the figure of a
woman was chosen as a possibility.
6
Thumbnail sketches of
Rebels departure from Bespin,
Ralph McQuarrie

1
*Matte painting of Millennium Falcon and Bespin landing port,
Ralph McQuarrie*
2
Detail of matte painting with live-action plate

2

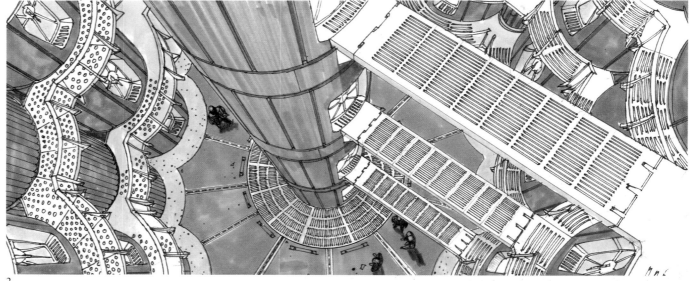

3

4

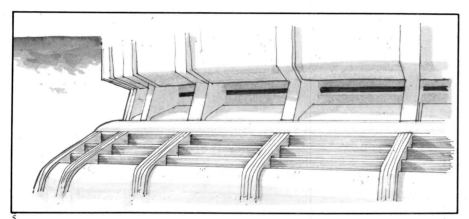

5

6

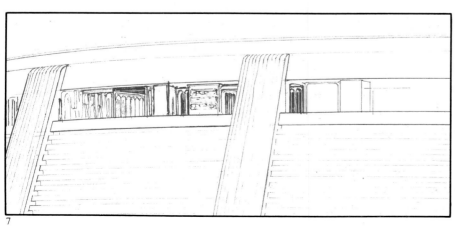

7

1, 2, 4, 6, 7
Sketches of Bespin architecture,
Ralph McQuarrie
3, 5
Bespin architecture, Joe Johnston

1

2

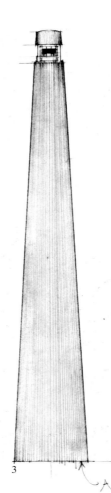

Production paintings,
Ralph McQuarrie;
A study for a matte painting, this
picture was composed around the
window area which was to be filled in
with the live-action plate from England.
In the film, Princess Leia replaced
Han in this shot. The sky and clouds
were added in the matte process.
Photographed with a blue screen
background, the cloud cars move
across the sky.

2
Han and Leia become suspicious of
Lando's gracious hospitality when
Chewbacca returns to their guest pent-
house with a damaged See-Threepio.
This room was described as being sun-
filled and central to four or five adjoin-
ing apartments. McQuarrie wanted to
project the feeling of a comfortable,
luxurious space. He gave the room a
sunken area surrounded with couches,
then added columns and metal framed
sliding doors that operate without
touch.

The design for the apartment set seen
in THE EMPIRE STRIKES BACK was
re-designed by production designer
Norman Reynolds.

3
Construction drawing for Cloud City
towers, Michael Boone under the
direction of Norman Reynolds

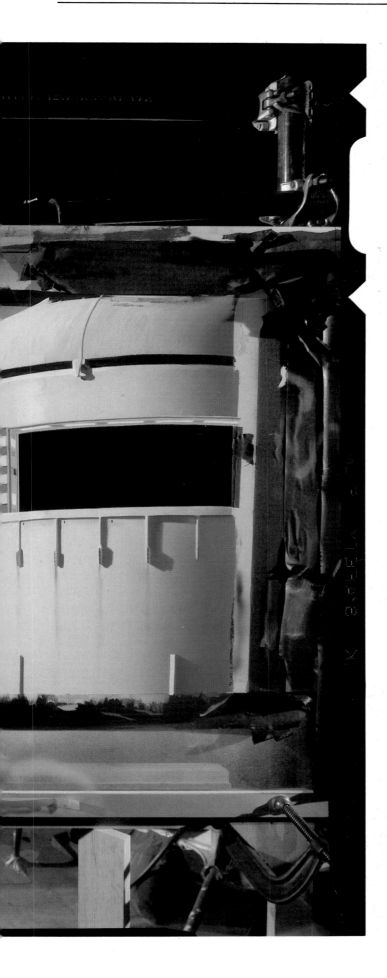

1
Matte painting of Bespin skyline,
Mike Pangrazio
2
Detail of matte painting with live-
action plate

1

2

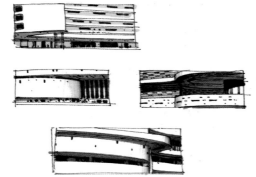

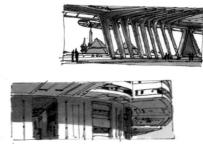

3

Cloud City / model builders note: sculpture and landing platform...
0357

Cloud City / main concourse
0358

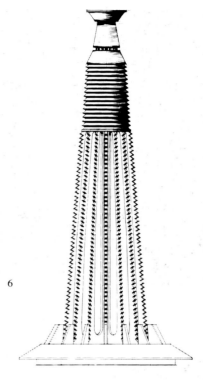

6

5

1
Production painting,
Ralph McQuarrie;
Lando stands proudly as Princess Leia
looks out over the cityscape. McQuarrie gave the upper deck of Cloud City a
cool, futuristic look. The smooth and
massive sculptured surfaces were inspired by the art deco movement of the
1920's. The round shapes of Bespin's
architecture set it apart from the angu-
lar shapes that make up most cities
we know.

This area of the city contains the ad-
ministrative buildings and the monuments to past great leaders. Figures are
shown coming and going on a broad
staircase leading down to a vast square
crossed in places by moving walkways.
A stickler for detail, McQuarrie even
gave the distant pedestrians shadows.
2, 4
Sketches of Bespin architecture,
Joe Johnston
3
Thumbnail sketches of Bespin
architecture, Ralph McQuarrie
5
Sketches of Bespin monuments,
Ralph McQuarrie
6
Bespin monument,
Richard Dawking under the
direction of Norman Reynolds

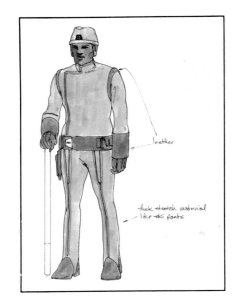

leather

thick stretch material
like ski pants

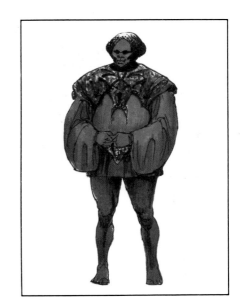

Princess
cloud city

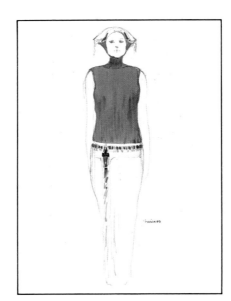

Princess

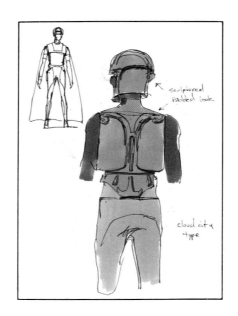

sculptured
padded look

cloud city
type

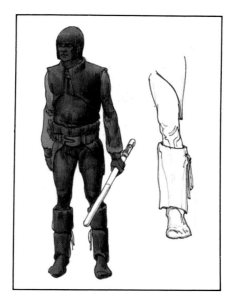

Costume sketches of Bespin citizens,
Ralph McQuarrie

2

3

1
*Matte painting of Bespin horizon,
Harrison Ellenshaw*
2
*Matte painting of Cloud City,
Ralph McQuarrie*
3
*Thumbnail sketches for bi-pod cars,
Ralph McQuarrie*

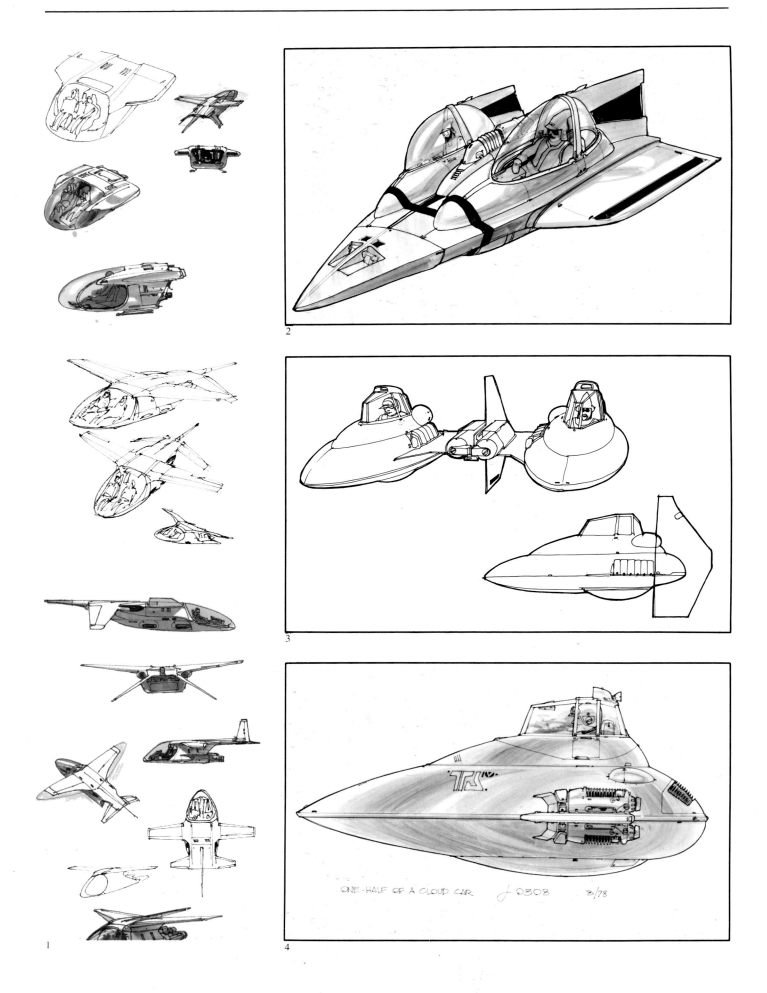

2

3

1

4

ONE-HALF OF A CLOUD CAR   0308   8/78

5

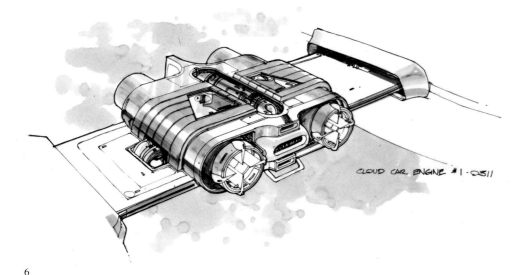

CLOUD CAR ENGINE #1·0311

6

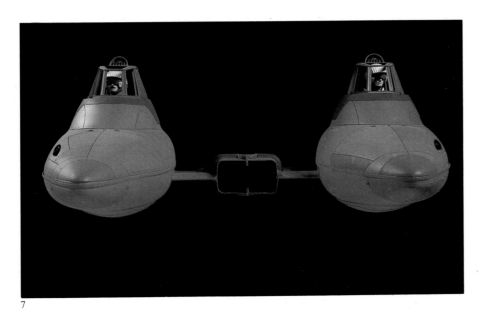

7

1
Thumbnail sketches for bi-pod cars,
Ralph McQuarrie
2 - 4
Sketches for bi-pod cars, Joe Johnston
5, 7
Side and front view of bi-pod
car models, photographs by
Terry Chostner
6
Bi-pod car engine, Joe Johnston

1

2

3

4

1, 4
Lando costume sketches,
Ralph McQuarrie
2
Production paintings,
Ralph McQuarrie;
This hall is based on a sketch from a series done to establish Cloud City architecture. It is high among the towers of the city. Clouds and other towers can be seen through the windows on either side. It is designed to inspire awe in those visiting dignitaries who are led through it on their way to meetings with officials of the city. The dining table was added when the room was deemed suitable for the first meeting in Cloud City between Darth Vader and our heroes. Vader, using the Force, will soon snatch Han's pistol from him and take the Rebels as prisoners.

In the film, the actual set was built from a different concept by Production Designer Norman Reynolds.
3
Han, now held in detention, has just come down the elevator to the prison area. Unable to see out of the elevator, Han does not know that Boba Fett and Lando have been bargaining with the Dark Lord over his fate. Warrior Boba Fett's caped costume is medieval in design. To the left, a creature-prisoner antagonizes a guard. Light emanating from the top of the shaft focuses our attention on Han. The bars of the elevator cast shadows out into the room thus heightening the dramatic effect of the scene. The doors, resembling old juke boxes, lead to the prison cells and the slots under the doors allow trays to be slid in to the unseen prisoners.

This design was not used in the film.

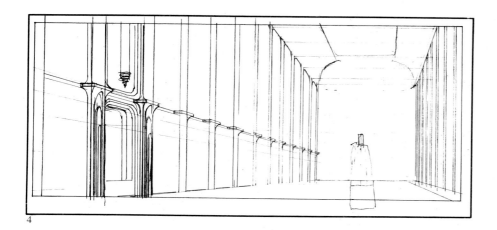

4

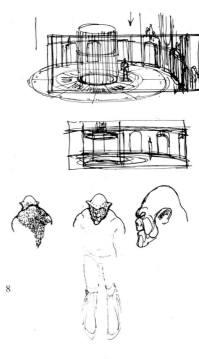

8

5

6

9

7

1-4
*Sketches of Bespin dining hall and
hallways, Ralph McQuarrie*
5, 6
*Sketches of prison detention area,
Ralph McQuarrie*
7
*Prison detention area,
Norman Reynolds*
8
*Sketch of prison detention area and
prisoners, Ralph McQuarrie*
9
*Early sketch of Lando,
Ralph McQuarrie*

1

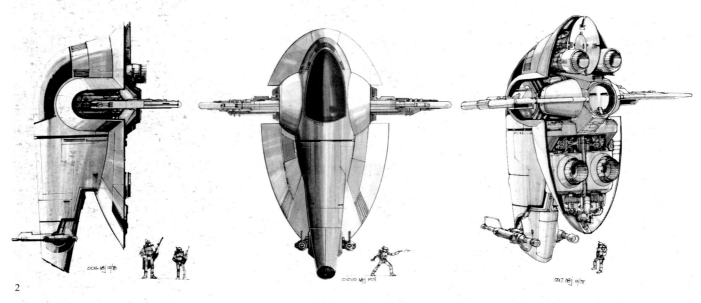

2

1
To depict one of Bespin's many hallways, McQuarrie chose the moment when Princess Leia and Chewbacca fire their lasers through broken glass at Boba Fett's departing ship. See-Threepio peeks out from the elevator, not quite ready for another fight. The appearance of Artoo-Detoo signals that Luke has arrived on the Cloud City.

This action took place on the landing platform instead of the hallway in the film.
2
Three views of Boba Fett's ship, Slave I, Nilo Rodis-Jamero
3
Slave I model, photographs by Terry Chostner

3

1

2

1
*Matte painting of Bespin landing port
with Slave I model, Harrison Ellenshaw*

2
*Sketch of Slave I on landing port,
Nilo Rodis-Jamero*

3
*Interior of Boba Fett's ship,
Nilo Rodis-Jamero*

4, 5, 12, 13
*Boba Fett helmet and costume
concepts, Ralph McQuarrie*

6-11
*Boba Fett helmet concepts,
Joe Johnston*

4 ◄
*Slave I model in flying position,
photographed by Terry Chostner,
retouched by Harrison Ellenshaw*

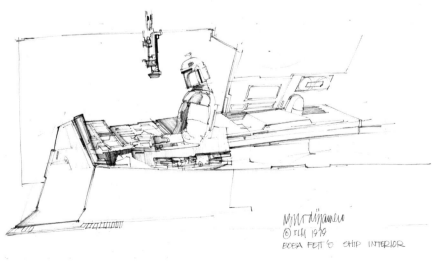

3

4

5

6

7

8

9

10

11

12

13

1

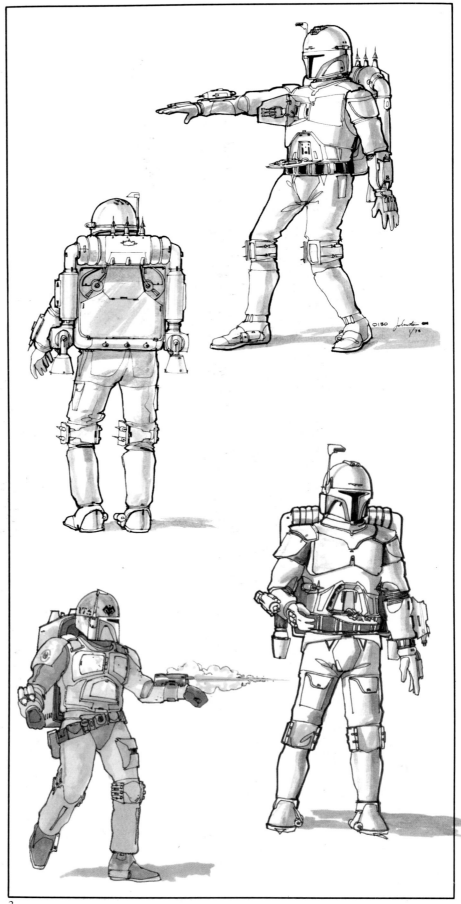

1
Sketches for Boba Fett's helmets,
Ralph McQuarrie
2
Sketches of Boba Fett, Joe Johnston
3
Boba Fett in action with sketches
of fellow bounty hunters. Sketches by
Ralph McQuarrie, photograph by
Bob Seidemann, airbrushing by
Ron Larson

2

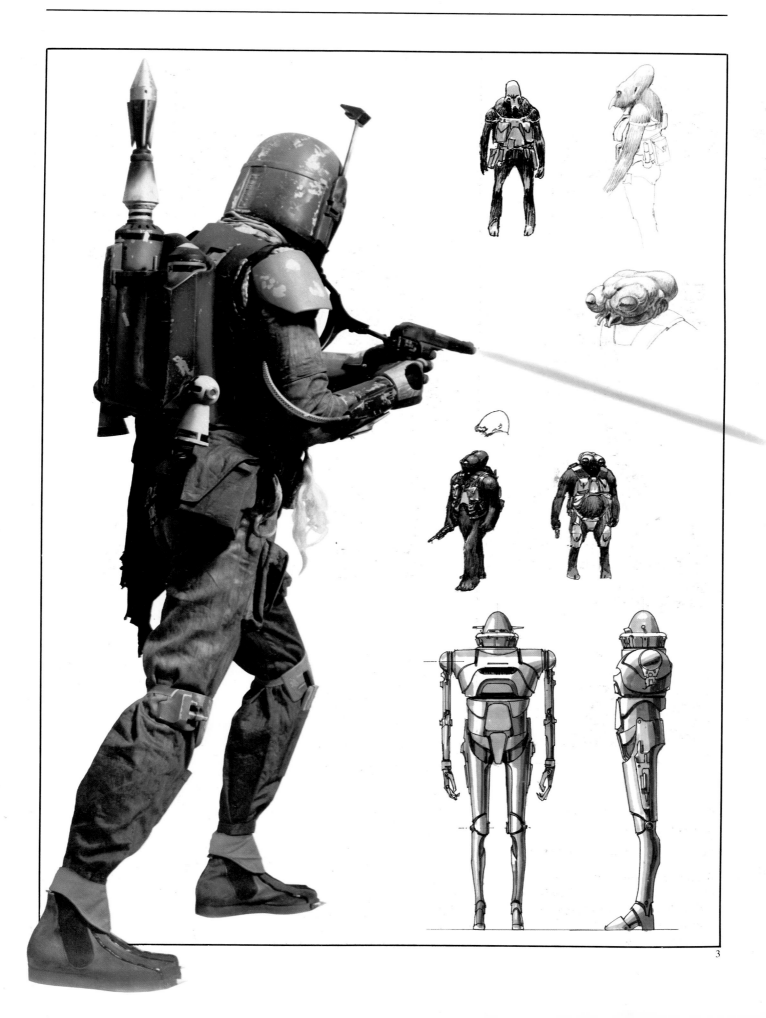

1

2

4

3

1, 2
Production paintings,
Ralph McQuarrie;
The carbon-freezing chamber is lo-
cated deep in the city near the reactor
shaft. Above is an early concept of the
stage on which Han is entombed to be
given as human cargo to bounty hunter
Boba Fett. A cold, blue light illumi-
nates vapor coming from the freezing
chamber below. High above are rails to
carry the carbon ladle and the great
claw which lifts the metal encapsulated
frozen life forms from the pit. The
trenches and foil forms of equipment
in the room were designed to provide
a place for the cliff-hanging duel
between Vader and Skywalker.

Later in production, designer Norman
Reynolds opened up the space to allow
for more dramatic possibilities for the
duel between Vader and Luke. Over-
head is an apparatus that is capable of
focusing a ray onto the platform.
McQuarrie painted this version of the
carbon-freezing chamber which
closely resembles the stage seen in
the film.

3, 4
Sketches for Ugnaughts,
Ralph McQuarrie

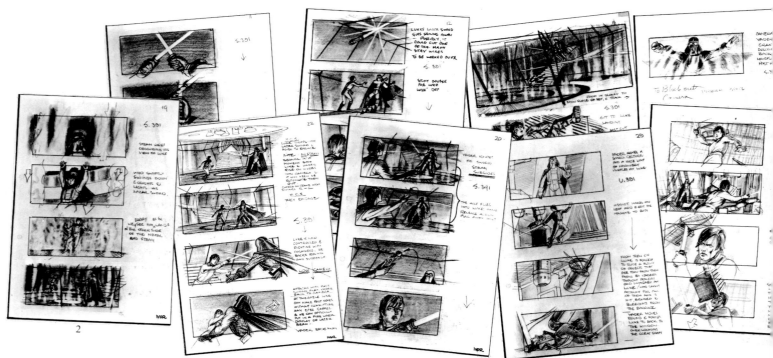

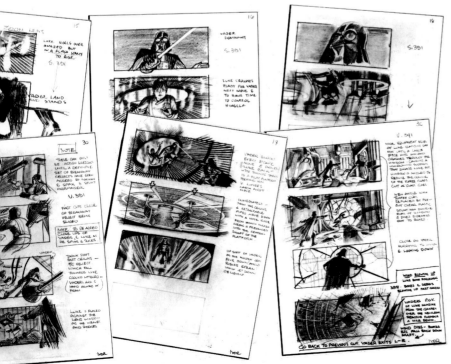

1
Production painting,
Ralph McQuarrie;
Enclosed in the spider-web structure of
the carbon-freezing chamber, Luke
Skywalker and Darth Vader duel. The
room is located within one of the many
vanes in the reactor shaft.

2
Storyboards of duel, Ivor Beddoes

1

2

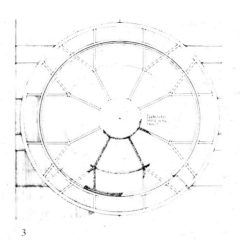

3

1
Production paintings,
Ralph McQuarrie;
This visualizes the moment before
Vader, using the Force, hurls a heavy
piece of equipment at Luke. As the
equipment smashes the round viewport
behind Luke, he is sucked out the win-
dow by a rush of air coming up the
reactor shaft. Through the window we
see the opposite shaft wall a half mile
or so away. The small lights are actu-
ally large ports for landing shuttle craft
travelling in the shaft.

2
The rudderlike vanes of the reactor
shaft are used to create desired changes
in airflow which control the city's
movements in space and route gases to
be processed. The shaft is about a mile
in diameter and is a structure which
houses a number of facilities related to
the manufacturing and processing of
tibanna gas.

3
Elevation of reactor control room
window, Michael Boone under the
direction of Norman Reynolds

1

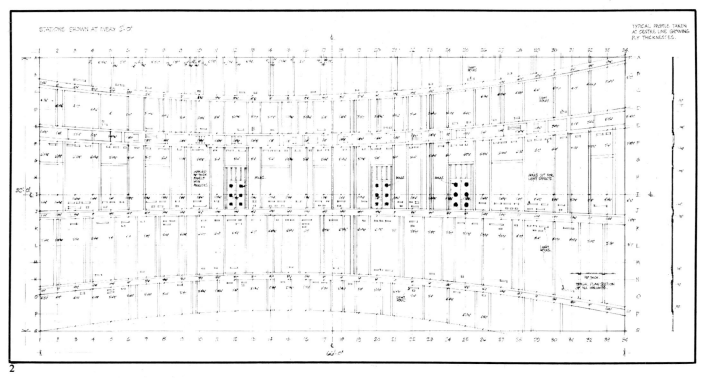

2

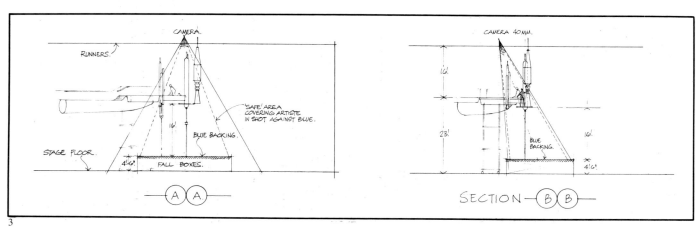

3

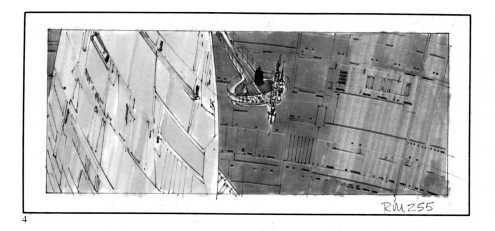

4

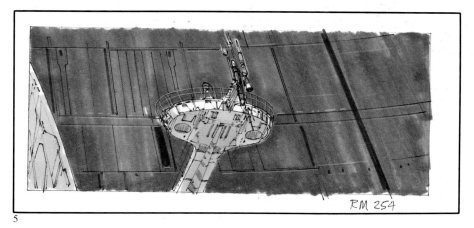

5

6

7

1
Production painting,
Ralph McQuarrie;
On the vanes' edges, projecting into the
center of the shaft, their cantileveral
platforms can be seen. These platforms
hold delicate measuring devices that
monitor the changes in pressure and
the types of gases in the shaft. The
whole complex provides the location
for a duel between Luke Skywalker and
Darth Vader.
2
Construction drawing of reactor
shaft wall and landing ports,
Ted Ambrose under the direction of
Norman Reynolds
3
Drawing for camera angle set-up of
landing port, Ted Ambrose under the
direction of Norman Reynolds
4-7
Sketches of reactor shaft locations,
Ralph McQuarrie
1 ▶
Matte painting of reactor shaft,
Harrison Ellenshaw
2-4 ▶
Matte painting of reactor shaft gantry,
Ralph McQuarrie

1

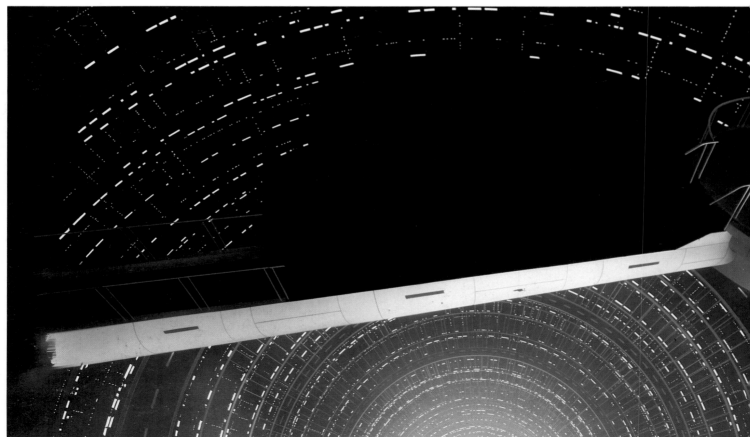

2

3

4

1

1
Matte painting of exterior Bespin reactor shaft, Harrison Ellenshaw

1

1
Production painting,
Ralph McQuarrie;
During the laser duel, Luke falls from
the vane platform and is then sucked
into an air shaft which leads to this
exhaust port on the underside of the
city. This painting served to establish a
possible design for the port and for the
fragile antennalike device which Luke
is able to grasp long enough for the
Millennium Falcon to swing past and
rescue him.
2
Camera angle set-up of Luke hanging
in reactor shaft, Ted Ambrose under the
direction of Norman Reynolds

2

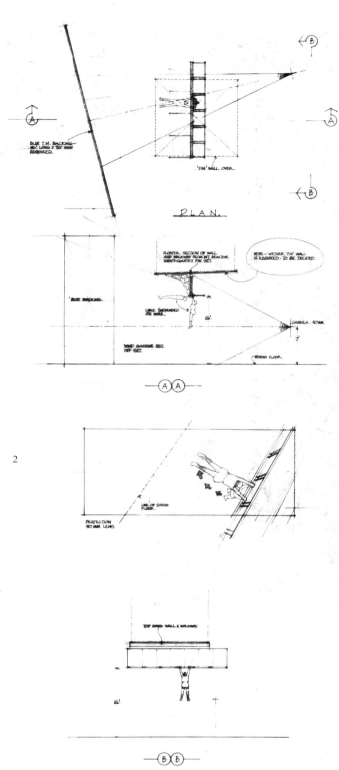

P L A N.

A A

B B

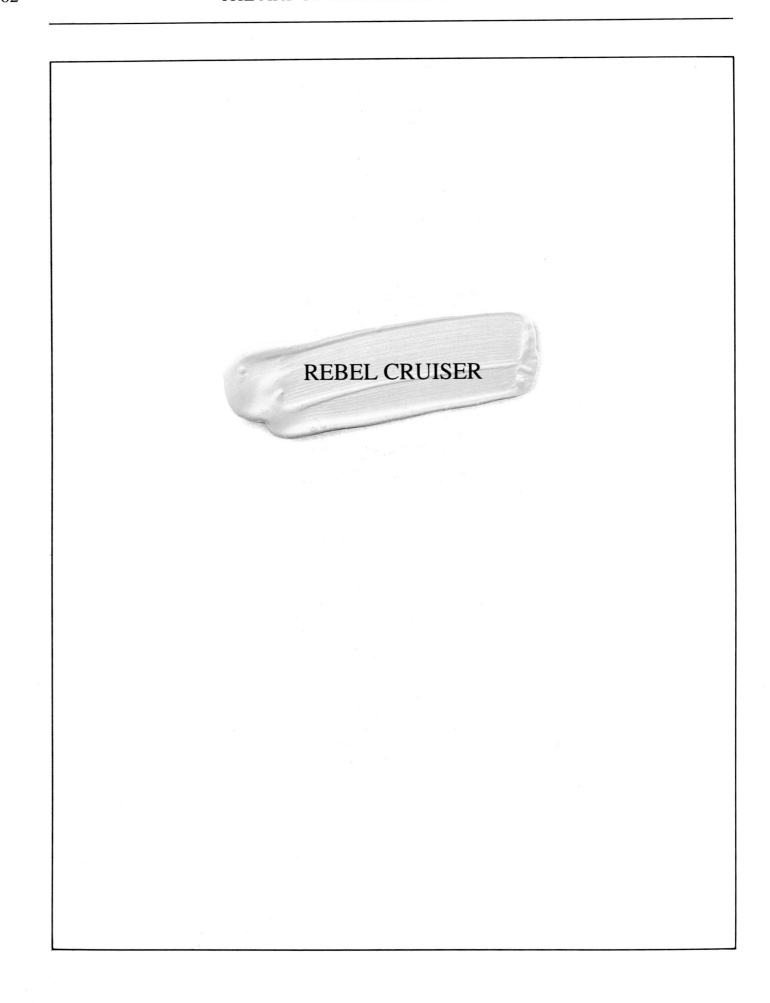

REBEL CRUISER

A Rebel Star Cruiser drifts in deep space at the Rebel rendezvous far away from any inhabitable planetary systems. Here, Princess Leia tends the wounds of Luke Skywalker during the short time in which the Rebels must plan their next course of action.

Each phase in the development of THE EMPIRE STRIKES BACK had decisive moments of spontaneous creation which enhanced the reality of the film. An example of this was the final design of the Rebel Star Cruiser

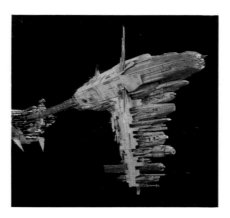

which did not change very much from the preliminary sketches done by Joe Johnston and Nilo Rodis-Jamero. When placed in front of the camera, the model's free-flowing form had a remarkable depth of field. Dennis Muren, lighting designer for all mattes and models, found that the fluid mechanical quality of the ship lent itself well to lighting. The Rebel Cruiser was one of the last models to be constructed.

When an idea captures the imagination of the people the way the STAR WARS saga has, it is evident that man's primal dream to explore and inhabit the universe has become a conscious longing. One day soon, in a reality not so far away, it is hoped that the nations of our world may collectively unite and reach for the stars.

MAY THE FORCE BE WITH YOU

Rebel Cruiser model,
photograph by Terry Chostner

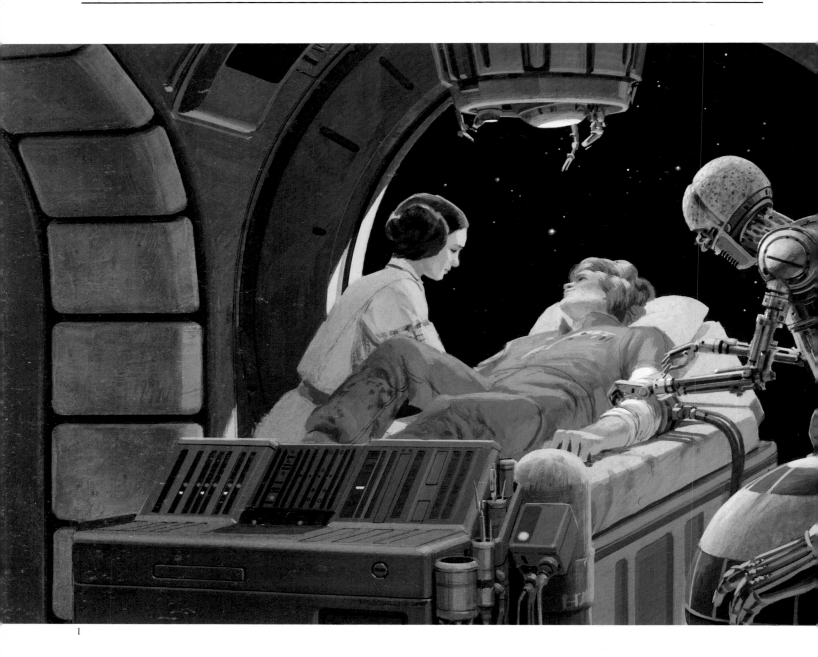

1

1
Production painting,
Ralph McQuarrie;
A moment of tender kinship in the
medical bay, See-Threepio and Artoo-
Detoo watch as surgical droid Too-
Onebee operates on the young Jedi's
wound. McQuarrie envisioned Too-
Onebee's medical staff as including an
assortment of support computers. The
unit at the foot of the bed is connected
to Luke's arm and functions as anesthe-
siologist while the optical unit over-
head gives the attending surgeon a
second view from which to make
decisions and a third hand for the
more intricate procedures.

1

2

3

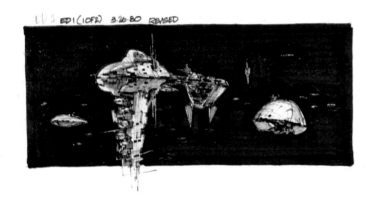

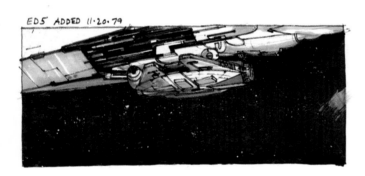

1

1
Storyboards, Nilo Rodis-Jamero
1, 2 ◄
Rebel Cruiser model,
photograph by Terry Chostner
3 ◄
Rebel Cruiser with live-action plate,
photograph by Terry Chostner

ED4, ED6, ED8 ADDED 11·21·79

ED7 (REVISED MAR 24/80)

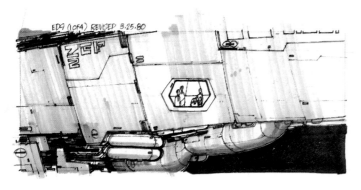

ED9 (1 OF 4) REVISED 3·25·80

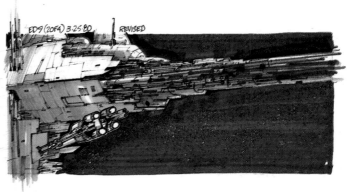

ED9 (2 OF 4) 3·25·80 REVISED

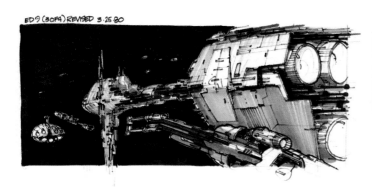

ED9 (3 OF 4) REVISED 3·25·80

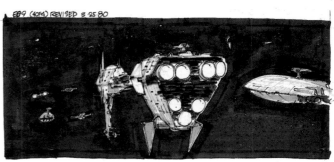

ED9 (4 OF 4) REVISED 3·25·80

1

1
Production painting,
Ralph McQuarrie;
This painting was done with the final scene of the film in mind. Luke and Leia look out a round window of the Rebel Cruiser as the Millennium Falcon, piloted by Lando Calrissian, goes off in pursuit of Boba Fett.

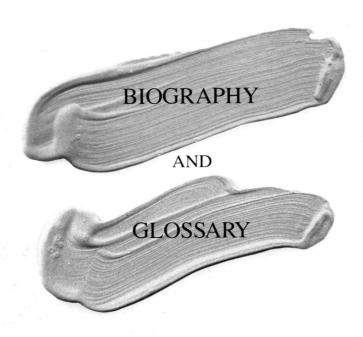

BIOGRAPHY

AND

GLOSSARY

RALPH McQUARRIE, Design Consultant and Conceptual Artist, studied at Art Center College of Design in Los Angeles and began work as an illustrator for the Boeing Company, Litton Industries, and Kaiser Graphics as well as CBS News. McQuarrie's interpretations of Apollo space missions gave millions of television viewers an accurate idea of what was happening out in space. George Lucas learned of McQuarrie in late 1975 and, very soon after, Ralph was at work on production paintings for STAR WARS. His other credits include CLOSE ENCOUNTERS OF THE THIRD KIND and BATTLESTAR GALACTICA.

PHIL TIPPETT, Stop Motion Animation, graduated from U.C. Irvine with a degree in Fine Arts. He then became commercial business partners with fellow Stop Motion Animator, Jon Berg. Both men continually contribute to the state of the art. His film credits include, an extensive list of commercials, STAR WARS, PIRANHA and now THE EMPIRE STRIKES BACK.

JOE JOHNSTON, Art Director—Visual Effects, is a transplanted Texan, who studied oceanography at Pasadena City College before enrolling in the industrial design program at Cal State Long Beach. Before joining the STAR WARS team as a storyboard artist in 1975, he worked on two science fiction made-for-T.V. movies, a remake of H.G. Wells' "WAR OF THE WORLDS" and "STAR WATCH." During the interim between STAR WARS and starting his work on THE EMPIRE STRIKES BACK, he did many of the designs for BATTLESTAR GALACTICA. An interpreter of ideas, he is an integral part of the ILM staff.

JON BERG, Stop Motion Animation, studied Photography and Fine Arts at Santa Monica City College before accumulating an impressive list of commercial credits as a Stop Motion Animator. Starting his film career with STAR WARS, he has since worked on the horror film, PIRANHA , and has been busy since 1978 working on THE EMPIRE STRIKES BACK.

NILO RODIS-JAMERO, Assistant Art Director—Visual Effects, new to the film world, studied Industrial Design at San Jose State before going to work for General Motors' Advanced Experimental Design Center. He then worked for two years as a Design Consultant on boat and aircraft interiors. His last job before joining Lucasfilm was for the F.M.C. Corporation, designing heavy industrial vehicles and military tanks. At ILM he collaborated with Joe Johnston on many of the craft in THE EMPIRE STRIKES BACK.

RICHARD EDLUND, Special Visual Effects, attended film school at the University of Southern California and the U.S. Navy Photographic School. His film credits include STAR WARS, CHINA SYNDROME, BATTLESTAR GALACTICA and various television programs and logos.

BRUCE NICHOLSON, Optical Photography Supervisor, was a Social Science major at University of California at Berkeley and went on to study film at Sherwood Oaks and U.C.L.A. He is now head of the ILM Optical Department. His film credits include STAR WARS, CLOSE ENCOUNTERS OF THE THIRD KIND, and BATTLESTAR GALACTICA.

NORMAN REYNOLDS, Production Designer, completed two years of national service in the RAF then entered the film industry as a draftsman in 1962. An ardent film lover, he worked his way up over the next ten years on such films as THUNDERBALL, KELLY'S HEROES and A WARM DECEMBER. This led to a prestigious career as Art Director on the films PHASE IV, THE LITTLE PRINCE, THE INCREDIBLE SARAH, LUCKY LADY, STAR WARS and SUPERMAN. Production Designer on THE EMPIRE STRIKES BACK, he will continue in this role for the George Lucas and Steven Spielberg collaboration of RAIDERS OF THE LOST ARK.

PETER KURAN, Animation and Rotoscope Supervisor, studied film graphics, animation and optical printing at California Institute of the Arts in Valencia and learned about special effects and optical printing on a special one year program at Disney Studios. An animator on STAR WARS, Kuran's other credits include BATTLESTAR GALACTICA, PIRANHA, AIRPLANE plus numerous low-budget features and commercials.

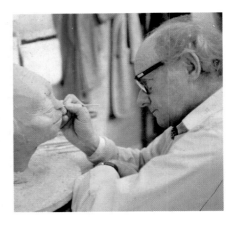

DENNIS MUREN, Effects Director of Photography, graduated from Cal State in Los Angeles with a degree in Business Advertising. His film credits include STAR WARS, CLOSE ENCOUNTERS OF THE THIRD KIND, WILLIE WONKA, BATTLESTAR GALACTICA, and various space education films and commercials.

JOHN MOLLO, Costume Designer, has written and illustrated six books on military costume. His widely hailed MILITARY FASHION 1640-1914 is a classic text on the subject. Entering the motion picture industry as a technical advisor on Tony Richardson's THE CHARGE OF THE LIGHT BRIGADE, he continued in this capacity on THE ADVENTURES OF GERARD, NICHOLAS AND ALEXANDRA and BARRY LYNDON. STAR WARS marked his debut as a costume designer.

STUART FREEBORN, Make-up and Special Creature Designer, began work as a make-up artist for Alexander Korda in 1936. He has worked on such notable films as THE THIEF OF BAGHDAD, OLIVER TWIST and THE BRIDGE OVER THE RIVER KWAI. A prolific artist, he is known for his make-up for the three Peter Sellers characters in DR. STRANGELOVE, the apes in Stanley Kubrick's 2001, and the now famous cantina sequence in STAR WARS. His recent credits include THE WIND AND THE LION, MURDER ON THE ORIENT EXPRESS, SUPERMAN and THE EMPIRE STRIKES BACK. He has just completed work on SUPERMAN II.

HARRISON ELLENSHAW, Matte Painting Supervisor, is an expert matte painter and has produced some of filmdom's most wondrous backgrounds. After majoring in Psychology at Whittier College he went on to work on STAR WARS, THE BLACK HOLE, BIG WEDNESDAY, THE MAN WHO FELL TO EARTH and PETE'S DRAGON.

LORNE PETERSON, Chief Model Maker, is the head of the ILM Model Shop and has a degree in Fine Arts from Long Beach State University in California. Specializing in science-oriented adventures, his credits include STAR WARS, CHINA SYNDROME, CLOSE ENCOUNTERS OF THE THIRD KIND, SPACE ACADEMY and BATTLESTAR GALACTICA.

BRIAN JOHNSON, Special Visual Effects, attended a public school in Great Britain and then served in the RAF for two years. Now a general in the ranks of cinema, a partial list of his credits include work on ALIEN, REVENGE OF THE PINK PANTHER, MEDUSA TOUCH, SPACE 1999, GLITTER BALL, TAMARIND, and THE EMPIRE STRIKES BACK.

MIKE PANGRAZIO, Matte Artist, started his film career right after graduating from Hoover High in Glendale, California. Having worked on television's MAN FROM ATLANTIS and BATTLESTAR GALACTICA, his work is now prominently displayed in THE EMPIRE STRIKES BACK.

IVOR BEDDOES, Sketch Artist, spent many years in the theatre as a choreographer, dancer, costume and set designer, and actor. He began his film career as a sketch artist on THE RED SHOES. As a sketch artist and matte painter he now has over fifty films to his credit including CLEOPATRA, DIAMONDS ARE FOREVER, THE SPY WHO LOVED ME, DR. STRANGELOVE, CASINO ROYALE, SLEUTH, THE SEVEN PERCENT SOLUTION, THE YELLOW ROLLS ROYCE, A SHOT IN THE DARK, SUPERMAN I and II, STAR WARS and THE EMPIRE STRIKES BACK.

Animation:

Series of still photographs or drawings done in sequence to appear moving when projected onto the screen.

Blue screen process:

A matte photography technique in which a foreground object is photographed against a pure blue background. The background disappears and forms a matte around the foreground when the blue color is removed from the picture negative. This allows a background photographed at a different time to be combined with the foreground.

Composite photograph:

A photograph in which various elements have been combined together on one piece of film to make a single image.

Front projection:

A technique that permits the combining of a previously photographed background with a new foreground without using an optical printer. A film image is projected through a front surface mirror onto a highly reflective screen on the same axis as the camera. The new foreground and projected background are photographed together by the camera. The part of the projected background that falls onto the foreground object and not on the screen is not an intense enough image to be photographed.

Full scale mechanical effects:

(Also referred to as live-action effects) Special effects that do not involve photographic or optical techniques, such as wire work (flying), robots, explosions, walls collapsing, steam, smoke, etc.

Live-action plate:

Live-action photography intended to be used as a front or rear projection plate to be combined with new foreground material.

Matte painting:

A picture painted on glass which is combined with live-action or miniature elements to create an environment.

Miniatures:

Models of vehicles or buildings used when full scale versions are not necessary or practical.

Motion control:

A process in which the movements of the camera and miniatures are controlled by a computer so that the programmed movement can be repeated as many times as is necessary.

Optical effects:

Any photographic effect involving the optical printer or composite photography using different elements.

Optical printer:

A group of projectors and a camera that permit the combining of many different photographic elements onto one piece of film.

Plastic arts:

Cinematic medium relating to model building and mask making primarily using plastic or related materials.

Production paintings:

Paintings done at the beginning of a film project which are used to illustrate important moments in the script. The paintings help the producer and director envision locations, sets, costumes and other elements that will be needed to complete the project.

Rear projection:

The process in which a film image is projected onto the back of a translucent screen and rephotographed from the front in combination with live-action matte paintings or miniature elements.

Rotoscope:

A technique in which a frame of a photographed image is projected onto an animation table. An animator then draws on tracing paper over the image. The traced image is transferred to an animation cell and is then photographed on high contrast film. It is later combined with previously photographed images to complete the process.

Sets:

Constructed buildings and environments designed to represent real or imaginary locations called for in a script.

Stop-motion animation:

The process by which an inanimate model is made to look animated by moving it a small amount for each frame of photography.

Storyboards:

A series of illustrations that tell the action of the script in pictures. Usually only action or special effects sequences are storyboarded but on certain films every shot in the entire film is drawn.

Thumbnail sketch:

Small preliminary drawings done before a painting or model design is started.

Trailer:

A short promotional film consisting of key scenes from a movie that is run in the cinemas to advertise a forthcoming film.